Neon 80s

Huw Collingbourne

MEMORIES OF A LUMINOUS DECADE

DARK NEON PUBLISHING

This Edition published 2012

ISBN 978-1-4716-0178-1

Author's web sites:

www.darkneon.com

www.80sempire.com

neon 80s

Inside

Welcome to the Neon 80s

It is the early '80s and London is the capital city of a new movement - a heady mixture of style and music; a new generation which has emerged from the leftover glitter and safety-pins of '70s Glam and Punk mixed in with a fiery electro-dash of Euro-disco.

At first nobody knows quite what it is or what to call it: some call it Futurism or The Cult With No Name. For a while, the term 'Neo-Romanticism' takes hold until, at last, everyone seems to agree that, whoever these people are, their collective name is: The New Romantics.

It started slowly, almost in secret - gatherings of young people in small clubs in London, Manchester, Birmingham and beyond. Disparate groups of young men and women in their teens and early twenties who dressed up for the hell of it, danced to a their own eclectic choice of music, and, eventually, generated their own musicians, and song-writers: Depeche Mode in Basildon, Duran Duran in Birmingham, Spandau Ballet and Culture Club in London.

They were an eccentric mix of ex-punks, gays, Goths, hard-core electro freaks, sharp dressers and soul-boys. The music was predominantly electronic, often with a heavy pounding beat and, sometimes, with more than a hint of funk and jazz.

Neon 80s

1981 was the year when this amorphous 'movement' came out of the shadows and into the limelight. The newspapers and the TV stations started reporting on these strange looking men wearing odd clothes and far too much makeup and equally strange looking women who were (confusingly) almost indistinguishable from the strange looking men.

Then another term took hold of the public imagination: Gender Benders. There had been men in makeup before, of course. In the 1970s, British 'glam rock' stars such as Marc Bolan, Sweet and Slade had dabbled in glitter-dust and eye-shadow. But the '70s rock icon who had played the gender-bending game a decade before 'gender bending' was to become a household phrase, was David Bowie.

Bowie was, in fact, one of the great gods of the New Romantics. You can see (and hear) his influence everywhere. It's oddly appropriate then that Steve Strange played a bit-part in Bowie's video, *Ashes To Ashes* (you can see him following in Bowie's wake constantly bowing as though to venerate him).

In *Ashes To Ashes*, it was almost as though Strange was auditioning for the role he was soon to fulfil - as the focus of the style, music and club life of the era. Steve it was who ruled over the small Blitz club (which gave yet another name to the 'movement' - The Blitz Kids) and, later on, the vast Camden Palace.

At that time, I was new in London and fresh out of a job. Thinking I might tide myself over for a few weeks, I phones around some pop music magazines and persuaded one of them (the now legendary *Flexipop*!) to let me do some interviews. Luckily for me, they liked my style and soon I was writing more or less regularly for a whole load of glossy teen magazines - *Flexipop!*, *Number One, Jackie, Kicks*, and many, many more...

I interviewed all the stars of the day - from Boy George to Simon Le Bon, Kim Wilde to Adam Ant. Those interviews ranged from the silly to the serious. The subjects ranged from music and style to love, childhood and (of course) sex.

In *Neon 80s*, I've collected together some of those interviews to recreate a slice out of time - that strangely familiar and curiously distant world of the early 1980s. Come with me back into the neon-lit, music-pounding night - let's make it a warm night in summer when the cocktail bars and nightclubs of '80s London are in full swing.

Ready? *Then let's go...*

Strange Days

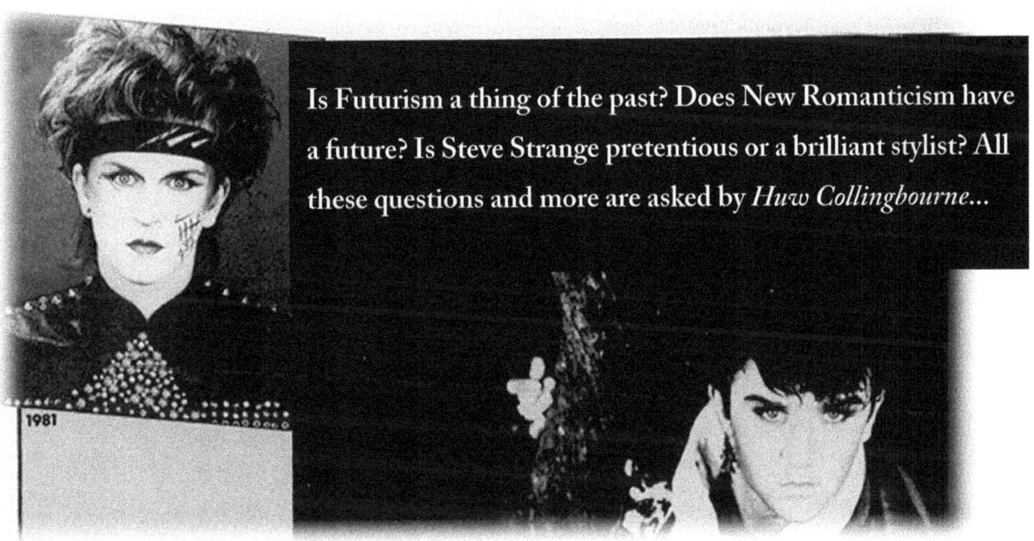

There is a sharp division of opinion about Steve Strange. Some say that he is a brilliant innovator and stylist. Others that he is merely a pretentious prat who's made a lot of money out of being with the right people in the right places at the right times.

A year or so ago I might have favoured the former possibility - that was at the time when, to a romantic soul such as myself, baggy shirts and synthesised percussion seemed to be heralding some sort of magnificent revolution in youth culture with Steve Strange as its flamboyant leader.

But now? Well, I'm not so sure. The music has become fragmented into a thousand and one repetitive variations of dance-floor electro-funk. And the style has become so exclusive that only oil tycoons and pop stars can afford to keep up with it.

So what's happened to the glam-idealism of 1981? Was there ever anything very special about the Blitz-scene in the first place? Or was it just a totally superficial six- month wonder?

"No, I don't think it was very superficial," Steve tells me, "A lot of creativity came out of it. A lot of the people who used to go to The Blitz have now become artists and designers - as well as musicians, of course. Even now there are new bands still emerging out of that scene - people like Haysi Fantayzee and Culture Club, for example.

"As for the whole fashion bit, well I think that too much emphasis has been put on that. The Blitz got so hyped up that you had to be dressed really outrageously or you weren't going to get in. It's true that I did vet people at the door, but it wasn't really that heavy. The barrier was because we didn't want people who were out to get pissed and violent, or skinheads or football supporters.

"I'll admit, though, that The Blitz did eventually become a clique and it was very snobby. But I've learnt a lot since then—and one thing is, you shouldn't judge a book by its cover."

If that is true, why does Steve seem to be so obsessed by his own appearance?

"I do give a lot of thought to my image as far as my videos are concerned and the way it's presented on the record sleeves," he says, "But I don't sit around in front of a mirror for an hour every day thinking 'God, what am I going to wear?' It only takes me about 15 minutes to get ready — and that's with make-up and everything."

I suppose it's all very easy when you've got a vast amount of money and cupboards full of clothes to choose from. But how can the rest of us hope to keep up with him?

"But I don't want people to copy me," he explains, "The reason I change my clothes a lot is because I get bored

with them. "I never wanted to be a fashion leader. I realise that fans have to have the idol-syndrome but I wish they'd do it in their own way. I mean, when I first started wearing suits I used to buy them all second-hand from Oxfam shops. You can get some quite good stuff there. Now, of course, I've got more money so I can afford to go to Anthony Price and have £200 and £300 suits designed for me.

"I still believe that a style or a look is intimately bound up with music, though I don't think that fashion alone can sell a record.

"There has been a lot of disagreement about my approach to style. For example, I had this notion to present the three faces of Visage. One was me through a cracked image, one was me as I am now and the third was me as a woman. Midge disagreed with that! He disagreed with a lot of my ideas.

"Naturally, I have made some mistakes. For example, I wanted to create a new look this year—like something out of 'The Lord of the Rings'. But it doesn't fit in with the music Visage are doing at the moment and then again it's too much like Toyah. Some of the pictures I've had taken will be used anyway because they've already been sent out, which was a mistake. But then, if people say they don't make mistakes, they're bad liars."

Being so much in the public eye, any mistakes which Steve makes tend to be gleefully seized on by the press, and he has become a favourite target of the gossip columnists.

"The music papers wanted to dismiss me after about three months," he says, "And as for the gossip columnist in Record Mirror, well, she adores me, doesn't she! A lot of it is libellous, but what am I supposed to do — break into their offices and tear all their copies to shreds?

"At one time Midge was going to take them to Court but decided to drop it. I sometimes find that sort of journalism offensive, but I don't let it bother me excessively. I've got over that barrier of being slagged off.

"These days I have enough self-confidence to cope with criticism. I have to, otherwise I wouldn't be where I am today. In spite of what people think, I've never had any financial support behind me. My father died when I was 13 and all his money went to his mistress. I'm glad, because it means that everything I've got now, I've done on my own. I like to be in control of things.

"Now that Midge has left Visage I shall be more in control of that too. I want our new stuff to move in a new direction. I want the music to be less cold. But I don't want us to go into that funk-orientated thing, which is so obvious. The next single we put out will probably be called '*Pleasure Boys*' —and that will be quite a change for us. It's all about sex, but it's definitely not done in the same way as Soft Cell might do it!

"The reason that Visage started in the first place was to break away and create a new form of dance music to be played in clubs—and not just traditional disco music.

"Obviously, though, that music can't stay the same all the time. It's got to develop."

Does this mean that Futurism, Neo Romanticism the Cult-with-only-too-many-names is finally dead and buried?

"I've always said that I never liked those labels," Steve corrects me, "Of course, the music and the club scene has changed a lot over the past year or so. I really think that it has improved immensely.

"London has become a talking point again in other countries, whereas before it was dead. And, in my opinion, that's bound to be a good thing!"

Is Futurism a thing of the past? Does New Romanticism have a future? Is Steve Strange pretentious or a brilliant stylist? All these questio and more are asked by *Huw Collingbourne* in this month's special supplement of . . .

...STRANG TALES

There is a sharp division of opinion about Steve Strange. Some say that he is a brilliant innovator and stylist. Others that he is merely a pretentious prat who's made a lot of money out of being with the right people in the right places at the right times.

A year or so ago I might have favoured the former possibility—that was at the time when, to a romantic soul such as myself, baggy shirts and synthesised percussion seemed to be heralding some sort of magnificent revolution in youth culture with Steve Strange as its flamboyant leader.

But now? Well, I'm not so sure. The music has become fragmented into a thousand and one repetitive variations of dance-floor electro-funk. And the style has become so exclusive that only oil tycoons and pop stars can afford to keep up with it.

So what's happened to the glam-idealism of 1981? Was there ever anything very special about the Blitz-scene in the first place? Or was it just a totally superficial six month wonder?

"No, I don't think it was very superficial," Steve tells me, "A lot of creativity came out of it. A lot of the people who used to go to The Blitz have now become artists and designers—as well as musicians, of course. Even now there are new bands still emerging out of that scene—people like Haysi Fantayzee and Culture Club, for example.

"As for the whole fashion bit, well I think that too much emphasis has been put on that. The Blitz got so hyped up that you had to be dressed really outrageously or you weren't going to get in. It's true that I did vet people at the door, but it wasn't really that heavy. The barrier was because we didn't want people who were out to get pissed and violent, or skinheads or football supporters.

"I'll admit, though, that The Blitz did eventually become a clique and it was very snobby. But I've learnt a lot since then—and one thing is, you shouldn't judge a book by its cover."

If that is true, why does Steve seem to be so obsessed by his own appearance?

"I do give a lot of thought to my image as far as my videos are concerned and the way it's presented on the record sleeves," he says. "But I don't sit around in front of a mirror for an hour every day thinking 'God, what am I going to wear?'. It only takes me about 15 minutes to get ready—and that's with make-up and everything."

I suppose it's all very easy

continued on next page

1981

1981

1980

1982

This is an interview which I did for Kicks magazine. It was published in August, 1982.

A Week In The Life of...

Marilyn

Saturday

Today I got up very late - about 4 o'clock in the afternoon! And I went straight out to do some shopping. I get paid on Friday, so I often spend Saturday blowing it all on clothes which I buy in the King's Road or Oxford Street.

These days I do my best not to get noticed too much when I go out, otherwise I'd never be able to get any shopping done. I don't go out in disguise, but I try to hide my hair a bit and I don't wear any makeup. In the evening I had dinner with somebody, but I'm not saying any more about that because it's private.

Sunday

I spent the morning at the recording studio then I visited a friend whose sister was going to Spain so we drove her to Gatwick airport. In the evening I had to go to a very long business meeting, so I only got back home at 4 o'clock on Monday morning.

Monday

I got up at 11.30. The first thing I do after dragging myself out of bed is to go into the bathroom to try to make myself look a bit more presentable. That means scraping off the remains of yesterday's makeup and putting on today's.

I went for lunch at Crank's Restaurant near Carnaby Street. I had an onion and mushroom pie followed by yoghourt. After lunch I went to see Colin Wild who is quite a famous tailor who makes lots of things for people in show business.

The last time I visited him I left a jacket that I wanted him to copy for me, but now I want to wear the jacket so I called in to pick it up. I walked down Carnaby Street for a while to see if I could find any clothes I fancied in the shops, but I couldn't so I went to have a facial treatment instead.

For anybody who's never had a facial, I'll try to give you some idea of what happens. The first thing they do is cleanse the skin, then they put a kind of thick wax over your face and scrape it off. Then they start squeezing end pinching your skin to clean out every pore. There are some other processes too, but I'm not sure exactly what they involve because I usually fall asleep half way through. By the time they've finished with you, you end up looking like a pig. It takes at least three days for your skin to recover, so I was really furious when I discovered this evening that I was supposed to be doing a TV recording the next day. I was sure I'd have big red lumps all over my face and I knew I wouldn't be able to hide them because you're not supposed to wear any makeup after having a treatment.

After the facial was over I had to go into the studio to finish off some recording. I was really horrible to everybody because I listened to the vocals I'd recorded the previous day and I hated them - so that put me in a very bad mood. I just went around moaning, "Oh, this is really terrible, I sound awful, you can't put rubbish like this onto a record." It's very unprofessional to go around grumbling like that and I know everybody else was getting sick of me, but I can't help it, I get really depressed sometimes when I hear myself on record.

The trouble is that, even though I'm very positive about the music, I'm very unsure about my voice. Actually, there was nothing wrong with the recording at all. In fact, I now think it's pretty good but that doesn't stop me worrying when I hear a new recording for the first time. Of course, listening to a track in a studio is different from listening to it on an ordinary record player at home. Studio equipment always emphasises everything — especially the bad things. I didn't have a chance to go out to eat in the evening so I raided the 'fridge at the studio and helped myself to some fresh fruit and yoghourt. Then I went on to do some more recording at the studios. I finished that by 2 o'clock on Tuesday morning.

Tuesday

I only got four hour's sleep so I was really crabby when I woke up. I had to get up at 6 o'clock in order to be picked up by a car to be taken to do some filming at the BBC.

When I'd finished there I went on to my ballet class. I'm learning classical ballet at the moment. I really admire the way that men ballet dancers look. Their bodies are much nicer than most athletes. Then I went to the studio again to sort out some business before going on to a party given by The Comic Strip. When that had finished I went on to The Palace but I got bored and went home after half an hour.

Wednesday

I went out for lunch with a journalist and my press secretary. We went to a really nice hotel in Knightsbridge. Then I went to the studio to record some vocals. Following that I went to ballet again. I try to go four or five times a week if possible. In the evening Kate Garner of Haysi Fantayzee came round and we called on a friend to watch some videos.

Thursday

I stayed in tidying up my apartment near the World's End in Chelsea. In the evening I picked up Kate and we went out for dinner. Then we went on to a party at Legends' Club. It was given by the boys of Westminster School; it was great. All the guys were in black suits and all the girls were wearing twin-sets and pearls. Kate and I were the only two people dressed differently. I felt like a pop star!

Friday

I woke up to about a million phone calls, organising this and that. Then I had a bath which took hours. Later on I'm hoping to go out if I can persuade a particular person to come out with me, but I'm not sure whether my plans are going to work out or not. Keep your fingers crossed!

Invasion of the Gender Benders!

At the time, there were no overtly gay pop stars. Not Freddie Mercury, not George Michael - not even Boy George (who famously once quipped that he preferred a cup of tea to sex).

There were, however, some very curious looking men; men who, frankly, looked rather a lot like girls: notably, Pete Burns, Marilyn and Boy George himself.

And when cross-dressing trash film star, Glenn Milstead (otherwise known as Divine) squeezed himself into a tight dress and huge wig to perform on the UK's famous pop show, Top Of The Pops, the British public reeled with shock. And the British press coined a new name - **The Gender Benders.**

Gender bending didn't just happen over night some time in the early '80s. There was, in fact, already quite a long history of pop stars who mixed and meddled with the presentation of their own sex and sexuality. David Bowie had introduced an unsuspecting public to overtones of gayness, bisexuality and masculine makeup way back in the early '70s. In fact, on the original cover of his 1970s album, *The Man Who Sold The World*, Bowie was wearing a long, flowing dress.

On the back of Lou Reed's 1972 (Bowie-produced) album, *Transformer*, there are two pictures showing (apparently) a man and a women though (maybe?) the same person and (just possibly, who knows?) Reed himself. Moreover, the songs on that album are full of references to homosexuality and transvestism.

CONTENTS

Pure Pulp for Pinheads

80 BELL ST, LONDON NW1 6SP
Telephone: 01-723 1395, 01-402 7535/8686

Editors Barry Cain, Tim Lott
Design Mark Manning
Editorial Assistant Leigh Bayley
Chief Photographer Neil Matthews
Contributors Johnny Black, Huw Collingbourne
Mary Ann Ellis, Robert Ellis, Debbie Hawes, Martyn Lambert, Dalyd Rees, Andy Boy Smith, Barry Spargo, Mick Wall
Advertising John Thoday 01-402 0121
Technical Photography Fabio
Printer W W Web Offset, Banbury, Oxon
Distributor Comag, West Drayton
Flexidisc Lyntone Recordings, Wedmore St, London N19
Publisher Barry Cain and Tim Lott for Colourgold Ltd

Subscriptions
Place a regular order with your newsagent to make sure of your copy of Flexipop (on sale the last Thursday of each month) or subscribe by sending your full name and address together with a cheque, postal order or international money order (sterling only) to: Flexipop Subscriptions, 80 Bell St, London NW1 6SP. Rates for an annual subscription (12 issues) are as follows:
United Kingdom £7.20. Air Mail Europe £15.00. Air Mail USA/Canada £25.00.

KISS & TELL

BOY GEORGE of CULTURE CLUB tells Andy Smith & Kisses JOHN MOSS

ALL RIGHT, I admit it. The idea of interviewing Culture Club's Gorgeous Boy George put the willies right up me. I mean, you've only got to look at him. A right weirdo.

Still, being game for a laugh *(and totally skint)* I braced myself and went, but not before I took a long, loving look at a picture of The Baroness I keep above my bed *(in case of emergency)*, just to reassure myself I was normal.

George stood in the sombre atmosphere of the Virgin press office smelling of something pretty queer, wheezing like an asthmatic smoker (and he doesn't even smoke) and stuffing a salad sarny.

"You look a bit young to be doing an interview," said George from beneath a black, wide brimmed hat. "Oh" I replied desperately trying to hit back with a spot of witty repartee. But being only 16 I couldn't think of anything.

Anyway, we left the record company and made our way round to the Portobello Hotel. Now, walking through the busy afternoon London streets beside this out and out freak ain't exactly my idea of fun.

Five minutes later over a cup of tea George talked about people's reactions to his bizarre appearance.

"Most people just say, 'Oh, look at that prat, what a queer' but when they get to know me they see the real me and change their minds - but I have had some rude letters recently."

Saying what?

"Calling me a filthy queer, wishing me six feet under and generally telling me to f—— off. I couldn't give a shit what people say about me. Besides, normality is a pile of shit. I think people are scared of being gay or dressing up because they're afraid of being alienated."

Boy George pauses to order a salad. In his multi colour Terry Hall trousers and black and orange Bow Wow Wow shirt he looked like a tropical bird. His face wasn't plastered with the normal amount of make-up. His eyebrows were finely plucked and pencilled in with black crayon. The dark eyeliner highlighted his green eyes that occasionally stared longingly into the bloodshot ones of our photographer's.

As he picks at his food George talks about his previous jobs - make-up artist for the Royal Shakespeare Co., male model, TV ad actor. Apparently there's loads of money to be made in modelling, "until they get sick of your face and decide they want to get some suntanned gits in."

It's really hard to envisage Gorgeous in a band. I mean, he ain't yer typical get it on-get it in-get it off bandelero.

"We try to work hard as a band," he said pouring out another cup of tea. "Not being the old fashioned, macho rock 'n rollers who are out on the road screwing girls all the time. That's such a lot of crap. I think playing live is an ordeal so I just like going home to bed afterwards and be without the screaming girls at your feet."

Girls? Did he say girls?

George never openly admits to being gay although he continued to make various witty remarks throughout the course of the interview vaguely directed at gays.

But enough of sexual proclivities, let's talk about music *(Makes a change I suppose. Ed)*. Culture Club's music bears some resemblances to Kid Creole, not coincidentally as George numbers the Cocunutty gang among his fave bands. The Club's last single 'I'm Afraid Of Me' bears out the comparison.

On the b side of 'I'm Afraid' the larynx of one Captain Crucial is highlighted on 'Murder Rap Trap'. He's a 14 year-old *(nearly as young as me)* white Rasta.

"It must be really difficult to become an all out Rasta because they have to eat the fruit of the land etc. White rastas are accepted in the black community here. But if you were to cut your dreads in, say, Bradford, they'd slit your throat.

"London Rastas are calm and gentle which is what it's supposed to be all about. I think violence is stupid. There's no point in aggressiveness."

So what would you do if violence broke out at a gig?

"Leave. I wouldn't do a Jimmy Pursey if that's what you mean. I'd just tell them to f—— off or tell the bastards to [illegible]. The crowd don't expect me to be aggressive with them because of the way I look.

"I think if more people were prepared to be themselves and admit that they're gay then they wouldn't look out so out of place. I mean, if you saw a bird walking down the street with her tits hanging out you'd stare, right? But if that was a normal part of day to day life it wouldn't worry anyone. Why can't it be the same with gays trying to be themselves?"

Pause for reflection.

"My last comment is, I hate sex!" Following that remark George threatened to kill me if I wrote anything about his, er, sexual tendencies.

He's not as bad as he seems, or looks. But George is bad enough. And I'll let you into a little secret. The other night he made love to

Pic: Neil Matthews

George and John: the odd couple

Meanwhile, in 1970s America, bands such as The New York Dolls, Alice Cooper and Kiss were going wild with masculine makeup. In the UK, the Glam Rock artists such as Marc Bolan, Sweet and Mud were wearing rouge, glitter and some decidedly feminine outfits.

There were also influences from the gay disco scene. And I don't just mean Village People. The great gay disco artist, Sylvester, whose heyday was the early '70s, was still a potent influence in the '80s. His one-time backing singers, The Weather Girls, scored a major hit with *It's Raining Men*. And later in the '80s Jimmy Somerville recorded his version of Sylvester's classic "*You Make Me Feel (Mighty Real)*". Somerville was, in fact, one of the first major pop artists of the '80s who was openly gay. Though the most famous "gay group" (even though three out of the five were straight) was Frankie Goes To Hollywood.

But in spite of some pretty explicit gay themes in songs and videos, Frankie Goes To Hollywood does not really qualify as a 'gender bender' group. The classic gender benders were those men in makeup who blurred the boundaries between the masculine and the feminine. These included men ranging from the immensely famous Boy George to the somewhat less famous Tasty Tim. Probably the most beautiful of all the gender-benders was Marilyn. And the most outrageous was surely Divine.

One thing's for sure - masculinity would never be quite the same ever again...

DIVINE DECADENCE

How did an ordinary Baltimore hairdresser, Harris Glenn Milstead, become the sleazy cross-dressing superstar, Divine, whose film and singing career encompassed some extraordinary highs (chart hits such as 'You Think You're A Man') and lows (eating fresh poodle poo in the film, 'Pink Flamingos')? I met Glenn in the bedroom of the fashion designer, Zandra Rhodes. Reclining in Imperial splendour, on mounds of satin cushions, he told me how he made the break into show business, with the help of his friend and would-be film director, John Waters…

Divine: We had already been making movies but it wasn't a money-making proposition. We just did it for fun. The first film I made was called '*Roman Candles*'. In that I played a drag queen. I was obviously a man in drag – I wore a dress, high heels, a full face of makeup, but no wig. Then, in the next movie, '*Eat Your Makeup*', it developed a bit more. In the movie after that, '*Mondo Trasho*', I had a blonde wig for the first time and I wore a two-piece, bare midriff gold-lamé outfit. It was when the look really started to get underway. And I drove a '59 red Cadillac convertible with fins at the back. I was a hit and run driver. In '*Multiple Maniacs*' I'm in the perverted circus. I went over to black hair. That's when the pouting lips came in. Then '*Pink Flamingos*' came along and the makeup really took off! Beauty gone berserk! Since then it's been toned down a bit. That was in 1969. But the films never made us any money – not even '*Pink Flamingos*'. And they were banned in Britain. Back in the '70s, '*Pink Flamingos*' was confiscated and burned. Then some cinemas started showing them late night. They put them all together in all-night showings. Well, if you can sit through *that* you can sit through anything!

Huw: Are the characters you play anything like you in real life?

Divine: Oh, God! I hope not! The character of Divine is like Joan Collins or Bette Davis – the kind of woman you love to hate, who'd think nothing of shooting men across the breakfast table. Divine was to be the most hateful of all those women. As an actor (though a lot of people would disagree with me on that!) I think the vicious characters are the most fun. When I'm in costume I feel I can get away with almost anything short of murder and robbing banks.

Huw: Do people expect you to be outrageous all the time these days?

Divine: Oh yes! When I get hired for a job, people say, "Well, Divine is going to talk dirty and wear tight dresses, I hope."

Huw: Do people get obsessed with the Divine character?

Divine: You bet! I'm having a problem with a fan in Germany at the moment. I woke up in my hotel room one day and she was standing over my bed. She'd bribed the hotel porter to let her in. It scared me half to death to wake up and find her staring at me. She wants to sleep with me. She calls my manager's office in New York three times a day from Germany, so I don't know what her 'phone bill must be! She doesn't speak English so she finally got somebody who does speak English to come and tell me that she loves me and wants to marry me and she wanted to know why I wasn't responding? She showed up at every show I did in Germany. It was weird!

Huw: Is she in love with you or the character you play?

Divine: Well, she's seen me out of costume and obviously she decided I was her type. When I'm dressed as a man a lot of women come onto me. I'm not saying I'm any Valentino but nevertheless they seem to find me attractive.

Huw: Do a lot of people find you sexy?

Divine: Extremely so. People come onto me and proposition me in dressing rooms after shows when there are lots of people standing around listening.

Huw: I don't mean to be rude, but aren't you a fairly improbable sex symbol?

Divine: Beauty is in the eye of the beholder.

Huw: Do people find your character sexy? Or do they find you sexy as a man?

Divine: I've been propositioned by guys and by girls, on and off stage, in and out of costume. More do when I'm in costume.

Huw: Men and women?

Divine: Both. Straight men too. Most of the people who've really come on to me have been straight, married men. One was in a club with his wife. She was drunk. He came over and started fondling my leg.

"I said, 'Excuse me, but what you see is not necessarily what you're going to get.' He said, 'Oh, yeah? So what? I think you're a really wild looking broad,' and he continued to put his hand up my dress so I slapped it, as any young lady would do, and I said, 'I think you should stop and go back to your table.' He said, 'No. By the way, what are you doing when you're finished?' I said, 'But, darling, I'm a *man*. Don't you think you'd better go back to your wife?' He said, 'No. I want *you*. If you'll leave the dress on, it'd be great.'

One man kept putting his hand up my dress. I almost broke his arm. Finally he put his hand up and *grabbed*. I said 'Now you've got it what are you going to do with it?' He was just holding on while I was talking to him. He was so shocked he couldn't let go. Finally I got his hand out of there and got rid of him.

Huw: After all the films you made, it was quite a change to break into the pop music business. How did that come about?

Divine: Sometimes it can be years between movies and stage shows. I was looking for something else to do as a way of making money. So Tom Eyen, the man who wrote '*Women Behind Bars*' and '*The Neon Woman*' – which are the two plays I acted in – wrote a song for me called '*Born To Be Cheap*', which I call my autobiographical song. And so I sang that. At first I would go to clubs to do Personal Appearances and it would last three hours. I'd change costumes every hour. I wasn't doing anything except sitting down, doing autographs and having my picture taken with people. I felt like an expensive 'Bar Girl' because I wasn't doing anything and people were giving me money for it. I was a bit like Santa Claus – having all these people sit on my lap to have their pictures taken. But once I'd done that in a club there was no reason for them to hire me to come back. So Tom wrote me this song and I wrote some material about things that had happened to me mixed in with a bit of fantasising.

Then I went to Bobby Orlando, who was the big disco record producer at that time. We cut a record called '*Native Love*'. Then we did '*Shoot Your Shot*'. Those records never did anything in America.hen we got a call from Holland saying 'You must come over here. *Native Love* is just entering the Top Ten and *Shoot Your Shot* is also in the charts.' I went over and then we got calls from Germany, Belgium, Sweden and Switzerland. The records had suddenly become a big success in all those places. *Shoot Your Shot* was even number one in Mexico for a while. I ended up doing a three month tour.

Huw: Are you deliberately sexy when you perform?

Divine: Oh, yes. That's the image of Divine. Sexy, but over-the-top sexy. But that's not me in real life. A lot of people confuse me with the character. I mean, I don't sit here thrusting my pelvis into your face while you're trying to talk to me (*Note: I can confirm that Divine did not do so during our interview).* It's just not me. I wasn't brought up that way. And in my own conversation you'll hardly ever hear me say a four letter word. But the character Divine will say anything! I was always taught that only very cheap people spoke like that. I was brought up in an upper middle-class family. If I said 'Hell' or 'Damn' I was slapped across the mouth.

Huw: When you perform on TV are the producers ever frightened of what you might do?

Divine: They think I'm going to stand on my head in vomit. But I wouldn't do anything shocking because I'd like to be asked back.

Huw: Would Divine have the same appeal if she was thinner?

Divine: I don't think so.

Huw: Are your dresses specially made?

Divine: Oh yes. They don't sell them of the rack at Harvey Nichols. Most women that size wear navy blue or black kaftans. The character Divine was always very big but considers herself very sexy. And to a lot of men big women are extremely sexy. I think I can look quite glamorous as a matter of fact. I have one silver dress, all sequins, and I feel lie a mirrored ball when I wear it.

But, for health reasons, I must lose some weight. I don't want to drop dead on stage because I'd hate to deny any of my fans my presence for as long as I can. I ate my way up to 400 pounds (28.5 stone) and now I'm trying to get down to 220 to 250 pounds (16 stone), the same as I was in '*Pink Flamingos*'. I had a sexier figure in those costumes.

Huw: Is there anything that shocks you?

Divine: I was shocked to hear bad language on British television. I don't object to it, though if Mary Whitehouse had been watching she'd have fainted.

Huw: What did your family think about your career?

Divine: They didn't respond at all at first. It

didn't go down very well at all. They're the type of people that think you should only be in the newspaper when you're born, when you get married and when you die. Showbiz was, to them, just vulgar and they didn't approve.

But as I became more popular they started collecting my press cuttings and I think they're now quite proud of me. Other members of my family – aunts, uncles an so on – think I'm terrible, a pervert, a hermaphrodite. So I don't see any of them.

Huw: You mean you've become the black sheep of the family?

Divine: For sure. My parents have become very open and sophisticated though.

Huw: Are you very self-confident in ordinary life?

Divine: I think so. I don't think I always was. There was a point when I was very uptight about being fat and I would always wear a coat and stand in dark corners and I didn't go out because people would call me names. I've tried to go on diets. I did get very thin – I weighed about 140 pounds.

And then my popularity grew and I said, 'Well, hey, wait a minute, I'm still the same person that I was,' and it didn't make sense to me. I never had all these prejudices when I was young. My grandmother was a very large woman and I adored her. Everybody else did too. I couldn't understand why my size should make any difference. People used to make jokes. Sometimes I can laugh but sometimes I think 'Now please, that really isn't funny.' And the people who make the jokes are always the people who should look in the mirror themselves.

Huw: Do you think you are very shocking?

Divine: Not really. The shocking things in the world are the politics, pollution and wars. The last thing that's shocking is a man in a dress!

Huw: What's the most revolting thing you've ever done in a film?

Divine: Eating doggie dirt in '*Pink Flamingos*'. Believe me, it wasn't my idea of a good time! I'd never do it again. I spat it out just as soon as the camera was off me.

Huw: What would you like as your epitaph?

Divine: I certainly don't want anything about dog shit! Please let me live it down before I die. Maybe it would be nice just to have "He made people laugh" written on my gravestone. Yes, I'd like to be remembered for that.

Footnote: The inscription on Divine's gravestone actually reads:
Harris Glenn Milstead
"Divine"
October 19, 1945

Pete Burns

says: "You wouldn't catch me dead or alive In fishnets!"

Want a to know a sure-fire way of getting Pete Burns really annoyed? Well, if you're ready for it, we're about to tell you - fishnet tights.

"You'd never catch me dead in a pair of fishnets!" Pete snarled, when we carelessly dropped the subject into our conversation, "I've no liking at all for the fishnet tights brigade - for one thing, they're just not practical and for another thing it's like a tacky drag queen."

And we always thought that Pete went in for a bit of tackiness himself. I mean, all that makeup, not to mention the leotard...

"All what makeup?" Pete snapped, "You may read in the papers that Pete Burns subscribes to lipstick and false eyelashes but it's just not true. I don't go in for makeup at all."

Oh, come on, now...

"It's true . I'm not heavily made-up. I'm just sun-tanned. I've got a sunbed which I use as often as I can, and there's nothing particularly feminine about a tan. And as for that leotard, it was an ordinary wrestler's one, and I've never heard anybody call a professional wrestler a drag queen."

As you may have gathered by this stage, Pete Burns is not very keen on being labelled with the 'feminine' tag. It's been said that he's just the latest in a line of 'Gender Benders', and some people have even dared to say (but not to his face) that he is nothing more than a Boy George clone.

"Anyone who's met me knows that's all a lot of rubbish," he insists, "I'm not exactly a petite little dolly bird. I'm very masculine. I'm 6ft. tall and quite a big bloke.

"I think all this so-called Gender-Bending is hilarious. I've always looked like this and until I got into pop music nobody even thought of putting me into such a category. These days you get record companies that think any man with a lipstick on is a potential pop star. It isn't like that. Only the serious, talented ones will stick in the same way that Siouxsie and The Clash are still around from the punk movement whereas lots of the hangers-on have faded without a trace.

"The trouble is that people are all too ready to jump to conclusions about anybody who they think looks a bit strange. They think you must be mentally subnormal. Over the years I've had to learn how to deal with people who refuse to take me seriously. That's where I learnt the blunt side of my character. I've always liked dressing up, ever since the age of six. I used to wear red Indian costumes or mummy's high heels - the sort of thing every little boy does. It's quite normal and good fun, so why do people get so upset if you dress up a bit when you get older? People expect me to be a feminine simpering little wimp. Obviously I'm not or I wouldn't have lasted this long."

It's certainly true that Dead Or Alive's music has a very hard-edged feel to it. And there's no way that you could say that Pete's vocals are 'simpering'.

"My stage personality is very aggressive," Pete says, "It's a reflection of my real personality. I don't use charm to get what I want. If I want something I simply have to go out and get it, no matter what it takes."

Pete says that he learned to cope with criticism the hard way - walking past building-sites on the streets of Liverpool - "I used to take a lot of stick from people whistling and shouting 'Hello darling', but it was a lot more good-natured than some of the bitching you get at so-called 'trendy' clubs."

These days criticism doesn't bother him. In fact, he sometimes goes out with the intention of being controversial.

"Well, people get so easily upset about things," he says, "Like the BBC got upset about my video for *That's The Way I Like It* just because I had lots of female body-builders in it. Really that was just a send-up of the sort of videos that people like Duran Duran make with all those models."

That song became a bit of a cult in America - especially in health clubs and aerobics classes. Pete appreciates that kind of success, because he's a bit of a health freak himself...

"I like to do some keep fit," he says, "I have an exercise bike at home, and some weights. With all the bad things in life, I think it's good to do your best to keep your body in decent shape.

"Although," he adds with a cheeky grin, "I don't think I'm ever going to be another Charles Atlas..."

Boy George's Testament of Youth

I was born on the 14th June 1961 in Finglas, Southern Ireland[1], but we moved to Eltham in England straight afterwards and lived in a cul de sac in South London.

[1] *Note*: Boy George later cliamed to have been born in Bexley or Eltham, London.

I spent a lot of my time at home with my mother and father, four brothers and a sister. At one time my mother used to look exactly like Bette Lynch in 'Coronation Street'. She had bleached hair, a huge stick-on bun wig and all the same sort of clothes as well. She looked hideous. But, at the time, I thought she looked brilliant. In fact, I wouldn't go anywhere near her until she'd got her makeup on.

School

I can remember my first day at school. I hated it. I hated being taken away from home and put amongst all these crowds of people. I still hate crowds.

They used to have a big bucketful of toys at school which we were supposed to play with. I didn't play with them though, because it seemed so childish to me.

One person I particularly disliked at school, apart from the teachers, was a horrible Chinese boy who had a snotty nose. He used to make me feel quite ill. Half way through the morning, we used to have a big crate of bottles full of either orange juice or milk. Just about everybody used to get the orange juice because the milk was so nasty. But I always got left with the milk. You see, I just couldn't bother to make the effort to run over to the crate and work my way through the crowd, so I ended up with the left-overs.

I've always preferred to hang out with girls rather than boys, especially when they are young enough not to be too aware of their sexuality. Girls tend to be more innocent than boys and also prettier. I felt that I had more in common with them - and you can make what you want of that!

When I was really young we all used to go to Church on Sundays. But then, one day, my little brother took his trousers down in the church and so we never went back again. I was very pleased about that.

In the early 'seventies, when I was still in junior school, I started to get into Marc Bolan. I loved glam, and I went really mad. I dressed up like Marc Bolan because I was so much in love with him. I grew my hair long, though my mother wouldn't let me put it in corkscrews.

Mars Bars

My secondary school was at Eltham Green. It was really horrible because kids at that age seem to get really cocky and violent. I started going round with people who were quite a bit older than me.

I had a girlfriend called Tracy, and another one called Ruth. Ruth and I went out together for two years. I hated her. I used to throw buckets of water over her and we used to stick

Mars bars in each other's hair. I don't know why I stuck with her. I suppose it's like getting married. Lots of people stick with people they hate when they get married.

I remember getting into trouble at school after I had my hair cut into a wedge and dyed orange. The Headmaster said 'Who do you think you are - a Belisha beacon?' I don't know what he was complaining about. He used to wear a gown and a board with a tassel!

The only teacher I really liked was the Art Teacher. He was a real lunatic. He'd come into a lesson and drop plates on the floor. Then he'd say "Now, I don't want you to draw any still lifes or nuns. I want real art". So I'd draw nudes. I was really good at it. I also used to draw Marc Bolan - not in the nude though. That would have been sacrilege.

Poof!

I was always getting into argument with the other boys in school. They all used to like playing football and I always did my best to get out of it by bringing notes from my Mum every day. They used to say "You're a poof if you can't kick a ball."

Eventually I got expelled from school because I refused to be caned for taking time off. Then I got a job working in a shop in the King's Road.

Looking back over my youth there's just one thing that I really regret growing out of, and that is the lack of sexual feelings that I had as a child. When I was really young I didn't have any at all and I wish I still didn't have any because they get in the way.

When you grow older everything is spoiled by feelings of guilt. You have to try not to hurt anybody emotionally, and if you do, you end up feeling guilt about it. You blame yourself.

I hate adult responsibility. I hate hurting others. That's the one thing that really worries me. Now we even get girls who come to our gigs and start crying. That worries me too.

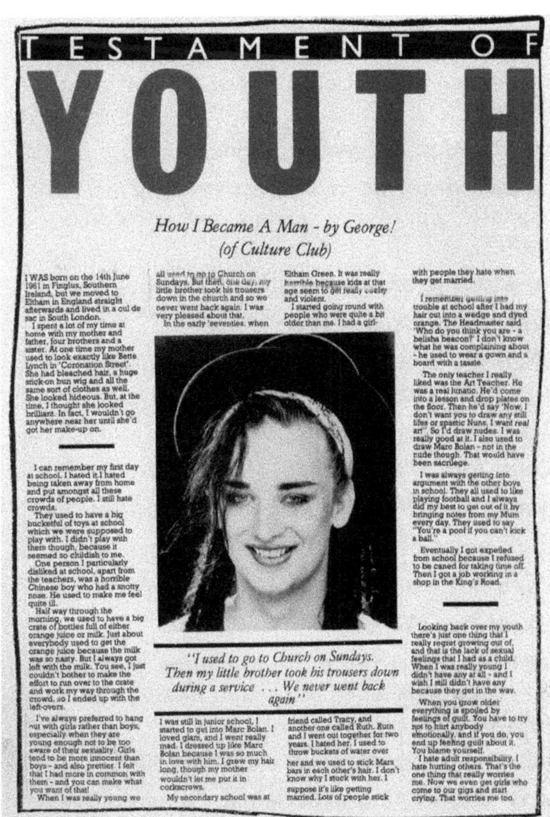

TESTAMENT OF

YOUTH

How I Became A Man - by George!
(of Culture Club)

I WAS born on the 14th June 1961 in Finglus, Southern Ireland, but we moved to Eltham in England straight afterwards and lived in a cul de sac in South London.

I spent a lot of my time at home with my mother and father, four brothers and a sister. At one time my mother used to look exactly like Bette Lynch in 'Coronation Street'. She had bleached hair, a huge stick-on bun wig and all the same sort of clothes as well. She looked hideous. But, at the time, I thought she looked brilliant. In fact, I wouldn't go anywhere near her until she'd got her make-up on.

I can remember my first day at school. I hated it.I hated being taken away from home and put amongst all these crowds of people. I still hate crowds.

They used to have a big bucketful of toys at school which we were supposed to play with. I didn't play with them though, because it seemed so childish to me.

One person I particularly disliked at school, apart from the teachers, was a horrible Chinese boy who had a snotty nose. He used to make me feel quite ill.

Half way through the morning, we used to have a big crate of bottles full of either orange juice or milk. Just about everybody used to get the orange juice because the milk was so nasty. But I always got left with the milk. You see, I just couldn't bother to make the effort to run over to the crate and work my way through the crowd, so I ended up with the left-overs.

I've always preferred to hang out with girls rather than boys, especially when they are young enough not to be too aware of their sexuality. Girls tend to be more innocent than boys - and also prettier. I felt that I had more in common with them - and you can make what you want of that!

When I was really young we all used to go to Church on Sundays. But then, one day, my little brother took his trousers down in the church and so we never went back again. I was very pleased about that.

In the early 'seventies, when I was still in junior school, I started to get into Marc Bolan. I loved glam, and I went really mad. I dressed up like Marc Bolan because I was so much in love with him. I grew my hair long, though my mother wouldn't let me put it in corkscrews.

My secondary school was at Eltham Green. It was really horrible because kids at that age seem to get really [illegible] and violent.

I started going round with people who were quite a bit older than me. I had a girlfriend called Tracy, and another one called Ruth. Ruth and I went out together for two years. I hated her. I used to throw buckets of water over her and we used to stick Mars bars in each other's hair. I don't know why I stuck with her. I suppose it's like getting married. Lots of people stick with people they hate when they get married.

I remember getting into trouble at school after I had my hair cut into a wedge and dyed orange. The Headmaster said 'Who do you think you are - a belisha beacon?' I don't know what he was complaining about - he used to wear a gown and a board with a tassle.

The only teacher I really liked was the Art Teacher. He was a real lunatic. He'd come into a lesson and drop plates on the floor. Then he'd say 'Now, I don't want you to draw any still lifes or spastic Nuns. I want *real* art". So I'd draw nudes. I was really good at it. I also used to draw Marc Bolan - not in the nude though. That would have been sacrilege.

I was always getting into argument with the other boys in school. They all used to like playing football and I always did my best to get out of it by bringing notes from my Mum every day. They used to say "You're a poof if you can't kick a ball."

Eventually I got expelled from school because I refused to be caned for taking time off. Then I got a job working in a shop in the King's Road.

Looking back over my youth there's just one thing that I really regret growing out of, and that is the lack of sexual feelings that I had as a child. When I was really young I didn't have any at all - and I wish I still didn't have any because they get in the way.

When you grow older everything is spoiled by feelings of guilt. You have to try not to hurt anybody emotionally, and if you do, you end up feeling guilt about it. You blame yourself.

I hate adult responsibility. I hate hurting others. That's the one thing that really worries me. Now we even get girls who come to our gigs and start crying. That worries me too.

"I used to go to Church on Sundays. Then my little brother took his trousers down during a service . . . We never went back again"

Boy George's Lifelines

Full Name: *George Alan O'Dowd*

Weight: *11 stone*

Height: *5ft 11 inches*

Favourite Food: *Japanese, Chinese and Indian.*

Favourite Drink: *Pernod and blackcurrant. Also water.*

Favourite Actress: *Jill Gascoigne.*

Favourite Actor: *Martin Fry.*

Film: *'Quest For Fire'.*

Record: *'Melting Pot' by Blue Mink.*

Band: *Madness.*

Person: *Jon Moss, our drummer.*

Best thing about being famous: *I don't feel famous.*

Worst thing: *Not feeling famous.*

I would describe myself as: *Sexually insecure, neurotic, possessive, loving and extremely manic.*

Worst thing about me: *Short temper.*

Best thing: *Good in bed.*

When did you lose your virginity? *I've never lost my virginity. I'm a man!*

Best gig: *Southampton College.*

Worst gig: *The Hacienda, Manchester.*

Heroes: *All the other members of Culture Club.*

High point of my career: *Yet to come.*

When not working, I: *Try to find work.*

Likes: *Being in love.*

Dislikes: *Big-heads and big-mouths, people who slag off bands when they don't understand how difficult it is. Adrian Thrills.*

School nickname: *Pouf, queer etc.*

Most frightening experience: *Going underwater in our video wearing all my clothes.*

Ambition: *To always be happy without hurting other people.*

Fantasy: *My whole life is a complete fantasy.*

Most hated person: *Sam from Maxwell's Silver Hammer.*

If I could change my appearance I would: *Do nothing. It's personalities which are ugly, not faces.*

True confession: *I'm a complete hypocrite.*

I collect: *Bad luck, ID photos, letters from Kirk Brandon.*

Most embarrassing moment: *I never get embarrassed.*

Worst thing that's ever happened: *Being in Sounds' 'Jaws' columns (the people who work for Sounds are wankers) because a cartoonist on the Evening Standard drew a horrible cartoon of me and I stuck it in his beer.*

Best thing: *Getting in the charts with 'Do You Really Want To Hurt Me?' with airplay.*

Criminal record: *Assaulting a police officer and breaking windows.*

Vices: *Drinking and smoking.*

First public appearance: *With Bow Wow Wow at The Rainbow about two years ago.*

Which newspaper do you read? *The Evening Standard.*

Secret fear: *None.*

Do you believe in God? *I don't believe in God as a full body but I do believe in the spirit of God.*

What do you read in the loo? *Depends which loo I'm in.*

What do you wear in bed? *Nothing.*

Worst illness: *Being in love.*

Spandau Ballet

Steve Norman Looks To The Future...

Ever since Spandau Ballet had a Number One with 'True' your music seems to have lost a lot of its energy. Don't you think you might be losing touch with young people just for the sake of appealing to an older audience?

THIS SPORTING LIFE

A FLEXIPOP Photo Spectacular

The Beau Boys of Bop Spandau Ballet reveal their hidden athletic talents to a clapped out, pot bellied, thirty a day FLEXIPOP reporter who smokes as well. From swimming to mountaineering to horse-riding the elegant quins from North London prove that they're just as fit as Seb Coe, Bryan Robson and Angela Rippon.

Steve

STEVE NORMAN – "I go swimming about three times a week. It's the best way of keeping fit closely followed by football and bicycling. I usually go to Parliament Hill or Finchley Lidos in London because they're much bigger than your average indoor pool. I also love scuba diving. Funny though, I've been scuba diving loads of times but I've never caught one yet. Slippery little buggers . . ."

Pix by Neil Matthews

If you take a look at a typical audience at one of our concerts you'll see that there's a huge mix of ages. 'True' obviously did appeal to some older people who might not have heard of us previously but that doesn't mean we're getting senile! Personally I like the faster stuff we do. I think we've still got more energy than most other pop groups. It just happens that our biggest hit was a ballad.

Spandau always seem to be incredibly concerned about appearances – the expensive suits and never a hair out of place. Just how self-centred are you?

The big problem is not being *too* self-centred but not being self-centred enough! What I mean is, the silliest thing we've ever done as a group is to behave and to dress in the way we thought other people expected us to rather than the way we really wanted to ourselves. I remember a couple of years ago, we used to go out in suits all the time, whereas none of us used to wear suits in actual life at that point. But we thought it what the public expected of us. Now we tend to please ourselves more. If that's being self-centred, OK, but I'd rather please myself than put on an act to please other people.

Don't you ever like to lounge about in a pair of dirty old jeans for a change?

My jeans may be old but they're not dirty. I wouldn't wear them to go out for the night but I do wear them if I'm going for a walk in the woods or somewhere. I'm not so vain, that I'd put on a tailored suit just to go for a stroll in the countryside.

Do you worry that you might get trapped in a style the way that people such as Adam and Boy George did?

You mean the way that everybody still wanted Adam to be the highwayman and George to be the boy in the smock and dreadlocks even when they were changing their image? Yes, that can be a problem for any pop group but I don't think Spandau have ever had that sort of contrived image so it doesn't really apply to us.

Not contrived! What about all the kilts and feathers you used to wear?

You've got a long memory, haven't you! Yes, I admit that was a bit contrived. But we got rid of all that pretty quickly and I don't think many people still remember our tartan phase. If we were still wearing the kilts today then we really would have problems

What's your opinion of all the image changes Boy George has been going through?

George has really got problems. Gary and Martin were talking to him the other day and they said he was in a bit of a state. The trouble is that as soon as George started getting some publicity he was put on a pedestal as being outrageous. But how outrageous can you get? You can't wear a dress forever and get away with it. George has really got himself into a tricky situation now and it's up to him to try to get himself out of it.

You don't sound exactly sympathetic...

Well, I'll tell you one thing about George - he's gone out of his way to lose himself an awful lot of friends. He does nothing but slag everybody off all the time. He bitches about everybody in the music business. There's no reason why he should do that. I hate it. He's a very insecure bloke, very paranoid. If ever anybody says anything about him he'll write a letter to the press. I don't think I have much in common with him.

Have you ever written letters to the press when people have said things about you?

I don't take the newspapers that seriously. I can only remember one occasion when I really did lose my temper and that was after I'd done an interview with one of the Fleet street tabloids. When I read what the journalist had written about me I almost went mad. He'd twisted my words to make it sound as though I'd said all sorts of terrible things that I hadn't. It was the typical sensationalist rubbish that you always get from the gutter press - and none of it was true. I wasn't going to write to the newspaper but I very nearly went round there and did something a bit more brutal. My friends had to persuade me to calm down. I mean, if I had picked a fight with the journalist involved, the newspaper would probably only have made another story out of it.

Do you ever have arguments with the other members of Spandau Ballet?

Naturally, but they're never too serious. There's no danger of us splitting up because we are very good friends and have a lot of fun together.

Do you think you'll be together still in another twenty years?

Maybe. If Status Quo can do it I don't see why we shouldn't.

You'll have to get your jeans a bit dirtier then...

In twenty years time maybe I'll be into dirty jeans and shoulder-length hair. In twenty years time I could be into pink frocks and high heels. You'll just have to wait and find out....

Tony Hadley's Lifelines

Name: *Antony Patrick Hadley*

Date of Birth: *2nd June 1960*

Family: *Mum and dad, sister Leigh, brother Stephen.*

What did you have for breakfast? *I don't normally eat breakfast but today I did have a cup of tea and a couple of biscuits.*

What did you dream last night? *I was so shattered from playing football the day before that I didn't dream anything.*

What's the silliest fan letter you've ever had? *Some people have written me some funny poems. Sometimes they are quite romantic but one or two of them have been a bit rude!*

If you could have one luxury, what would you choose? *A case full of twenty pound notes - up to about a million pounds.*

Have you ever been in hospital? *Yes. I had a disease of the bone marrow about twelve years ago. I was in for about two months and when I finally came out I had to go about on crutches.*

Any gory details? *They had to drill into my bones and draw fluid off. I also had to have jabs up my backside - which was not very nice.*

Phobias? *Beetles. I hate them.*

What's the silliest item of clothing you've ever worn? *I went to a toga party once wearing hob-nailed boots, a crash helmet and a sheet.*

If you could be any fictional character, which would you choose? *Harrison Ford in 'Raiders of the Lost Ark'.*

If you had one day to love, how would you spend it? *Miserably.*

Who would you like to be marooned on a desert island with? *Max Bygraves.*

Depeche mode

Welcome To The Working Week

Seven Days In The Life of Dave 'Have A Banana' Gahan

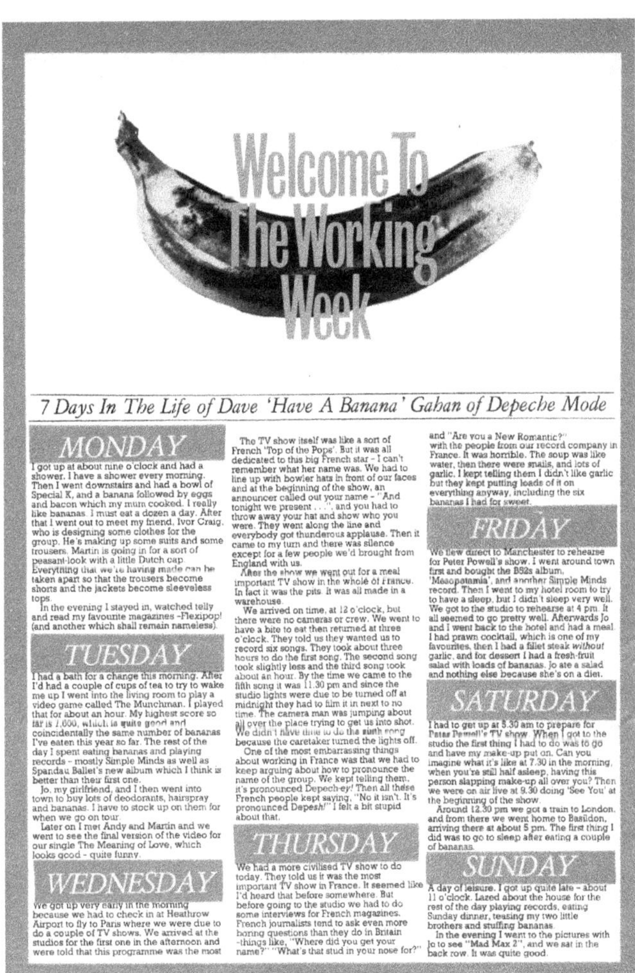

7 Days In The Life of Dave 'Have A Banana' Gahan of Depeche Mode

MONDAY

I got up at about nine o'clock and had a shower. I have a shower every morning. Then I went downstairs and had a bowl of Special K, and a banana followed by eggs and bacon which my mum cooked. I really like bananas. I must eat a dozen a day. After that I went out to meet my friend, Ivor Craig, who is designing some clothes for the group. He's making up some suits and some trousers. Martin is going in for a sort of peasant-look with a little Dutch cap. Everything that we're having made can be taken apart so that the trousers become shorts and the jackets become sleeveless tops.

In the evening I stayed in, watched telly and read my favourite magazines -Flexipop! (and another which shall remain nameless).

TUESDAY

I had a bath for a change this morning. After I'd had a couple of cups of tea to try to wake me up I went into the living room to play a video game called The Munchman. I played that for about an hour. My highest score so far is 7,600, which is quite good and coincidentally the same number of bananas I've eaten this year so far. The rest of the day I spent eating bananas and playing records - mostly Simple Minds as well as Spandau Ballet's new album which I think is better than their first one.

Jo, my girlfriend, and I then went into town to buy lots of deodorants, hairspray and bananas. I have to stock up on them for when we go on tour.

Later on I met Andy and Martin and we went to see the final version of the video for our single The Meaning of Love, which looks good - quite funny.

WEDNESDAY

We got up very early in the morning because we had to check in at Heathrow Airport to fly to Paris where we were due to do a couple of TV shows. We arrived at the studios for the first one in the afternoon and were told that this programme was the most

The TV show itself was like a sort of French 'Top of the Pops'. But it was all dedicated to this big French star - I can't remember what her name was. We had to line up with bowler hats in front of our faces and at the beginning of the show, an announcer called out your name - "And tonight we present . . .", and you had to throw away your hat and show who you were. They went along the line and everybody got thunderous applause. Then it came to my turn and there was silence except for a few people we'd brought from England with us.

After the show we went out for a meal important TV show in the whole of France. In fact it was the pits. It was all made in a warehouse.

We arrived on time, at 12 o'clock, but there were no cameras or crew. We went to have a bite to eat then returned at three o'clock. They told us they wanted us to record six songs. They took about three hours to do the first song. The second song took slightly less and the third song took about an hour. By the time we came to the fifth song it was 11.30 pm and since the studio lights were due to be turned off at midnight they had to film it in next to no time. The camera man was jumping about all over the place trying to get us into shot. We didn't have time to do the sixth song because the caretaker turned the lights off.

One of the most embarrassing things about working in France was that we had to keep arguing about how to pronounce the name of the group. We kept telling them, it's pronounced Depech-*ey*! Then all these French people kept saying, "No it isn't. It's pronounced Depe*sh*!" I felt a bit stupid about that.

THURSDAY

We had a more civilised TV show to do today. They told us it was the most important TV show in France. It seemed like I'd heard that before somewhere. But before going to the studio we had to do some interviews for French magazines. French journalists tend to ask even more boring questions than they do in Britain -things like, "Where did you get your name?" "What's that stud in your nose for?" and "Are you a New Romantic?" with the people from our record company in France. It was horrible. The soup was like water, then there were snails, and lots of garlic. I kept telling them I didn't like garlic but they kept putting loads of it on everything anyway, including the six bananas I had for sweet.

FRIDAY

We flew direct to Manchester to rehearse for Peter Powell's show. I went around town first and bought the B52s album, 'Mesopotamia', and another Simple Minds record. Then I went to my hotel room to try to have a sleep, but I didn't sleep very well. We got to the studio to rehearse at 4 pm. It all seemed to go pretty well. Afterwards Jo and I went back to the hotel and had a meal. I had prawn cocktail, which is one of my favourites, then I had a fillet steak *without* garlic, and for dessert I had a fresh-fruit salad with loads of bananas. Jo ate a salad and nothing else because she's on a diet.

SATURDAY

I had to get up at 5.30 am to prepare for Peter Powell's TV show. When I got to the studio the first thing I had to do was to go and have my make-up put on. Can you imagine what it's like at 7.30 in the morning, when you're still half asleep, having this person slapping make-up all over you? Then we were on air live at 9.30 doing 'See You' at the beginning of the show.

Around 12.30 pm we got a train to London, and from there we went home to Basildon, arriving there at about 5 pm. The first thing I did was to go to sleep after eating a couple of bananas.

SUNDAY

A day of leisure. I got up quite late - about 11 o'clock. Lazed about the house for the rest of the day playing records, eating Sunday dinner, teasing my two little brothers and stuffing bananas.

In the evening I went to the pictures with Jo to see "Mad Max 2", and we sat in the back row. It was quite good.

Monday

I got up at about nine o'clock and had a shower. I have a shower every morning. Then I went downstairs and had a bowl of Special K and a banana followed by eggs and bacon which my mum cooked. I really like bananas. I must eat a dozen a day. After that I went out to meet my friend, Ivor Craig, who is designing some clothes for the group. He's making up some suits and some trousers. Martin is going in for a sort of peasant-look with a little Dutch cap. Everything that we're having made can be taken apart so that the trousers become shorts and the jackets become sleeveless tops. In the evening I stayed in, watched telly and read my favourite magazines - *Flexipop*! (and another which shall remain nameless).

Tuesday

I had a bath for a change this morning. After I'd had a couple of cups of tea to try to wake me up I went into the living room to play a video game called *The Munchman*. I played that for about an hour. My highest score so far is 7,600, which is quite good and coincidentally the same number of bananas

I've eaten this year so far. The rest of the day I spent eating bananas and playing records - mostly Simple Minds as well as Spandau Ballet's new album which I think is better than their first one. Jo, my girlfriend, and I then went into town to buy lots of deodorants, hairspray and bananas. I have to stock up on them for when we go on tour. Later on I met Andy and Martin and we went to see the final version of the video for our single *The Meaning of Love*, which looks good - quite funny.

Wednesday

We got up very early in the morning because we had to check in at Heathrow Airport to fly to Paris where we were due to do a couple of TV shows. We arrived at the studios for the first one in the afternoon and were told that this programme was the most important TV show in the whole of France. In fact it was the pits. It was all made in a warehouse. The TV show itself was like a sort of French 'Top of the Pops'. But it was all dedicated to this big French star - I can't remember what her name was. We had to line up with bowler hats in front of our faces and at the beginning of the show, an announcer called out your name - "And tonight we present...", and you had to throw away your hat and show who you were. They went along the line and everybody got thunderous applause. Then it came to my turn and there was silence except for a few people we'd brought from England with us. We arrived on time, at 12 o'clock, but there were no cameras or crew. We went to have a bite to eat then returned at three o'clock. They told us they wanted us to record six songs. They took about three hours to do the first song. The second song took slightly less and the third song took about an hour. By the time we came to the fifth song it was 11.30 pm and since the studio lights were due to be turned off at midnight they had to film it in next to no time. The camera man was jumping about all over the place trying to get us into shot. We didn't have time to do the sixth song because the caretaker turned the lights off. One of the most embarrassing things about working in France was that we had to keep arguing about how to pronounce the name of the group. We kept telling them, it's pronounced Depech-*ey*! Then all these French people kept saying, "No it isn't. It's pronounced Depesh!" I felt a bit stupid about that.

Thursday

We had a more civilised TV show to do today. They told us it was the most important TV show in France. It seemed like I'd heard that before somewhere. But before going to the studio we had to do some interviews for French magazines. French journalists tend to ask even more boring questions than they do in Britain -things like Where did you get your name? What's that stud in your nose for? and "Are you a New Romantic?" After the show we went to dinner with the people from our record company in France. It was horrible. The soup was like water, then there were snails, and lots of garlic. I kept telling them I didn't like garlic but they kept putting loads of it on everything anyway, including the six bananas I had for sweet.

Friday

We flew direct to Manchester to rehearse for Peter Powell's show. I went around town first and bought the B52s album, *'Mesopotamia'*, and another Simple Minds record. Then I went to my hotel room to try to have a sleep, but I didn't sleep very well. We got to the studio to rehearse at 4 pm. It all seemed to go pretty well. Afterwards Jo and I went back to the hotel and had a meal. I had prawn cocktail, which is one of my favourites, then I had a fillet steak without garlic, and for dessert I had a fresh-fruit salad with loads of bananas. Jo ate a salad and nothing else because she's on a diet.

Saturday

I had to get up at 5.30am to prepare for Peter Powell's TV show. When I got to the studio the first thing I had to do was to go and have my makeup put on. Can you imagine what it's like at 7.30 in the morning, when you're still half asleep, having this person slapping makeup all over you? Then we were on air live at 9.30 doing 'See You' at the beginning of the show. Around 12.30 pm we got a train to London, and from there we went home to Basildon, arriving there at about 5pm. The first thing I did was to go to sleep after eating a couple of bananas.

Sunday

A day of leisure. I got up quite late - about 11 o'clock. Lazed about the house for the rest of the day playing records, eating Sunday dinner, teasing my two little brothers - and stuffing bananas.

In the evening I went to the pictures with Jo to see "*Mad Max 2*", and we sat in the back row. It was quite good.

Does Dave really have a banana obsession or did we make it all up for the sake of a silly photo? I'm not saying...

LIMAHL

MUSCLEBOUND

...in which I get down to the flesh of the Kajagoogoo lead singer...

Limahl, I was confidently informed, is destined to be The Next Big Heart-Throb. In comparison with his sultry good-looks, Simon le Bon would seem about as erotic as a middle-aged Irish navvy with a hernia, David Sylvian would look like a runner-up in a glamorous grannie competition, and Steve Strange would look like, well...Steve Strange.

I settled myself in a sumptuous settee in the offices of Limahl's record company, EMI, and tremulously awaited his arrival. Long seconds passed, and then, as is their wont, even longer minutes.

The appointed time drew nearer and my pulse began to race, a cold sweat stood out upon my brow and an electric thrill of highly questionable sexuality tingled through every sinew of my body.

MUSCLEBOUND

Silly name, but high in the charts. HUW COLLINGBOURNE pumps iron with KAJAGOOGOO'S muscle-man LIMAHL...

LIMAHL, I was confidently informed, is destined to be The Next Big Heart-Throb. In comparison with his sultry good-looks, Simon le Bon would seem about as erotic as a middle-aged Irish navvy with a hernia, David Sylvian would look like a runner-up in a glamorous grannie competition, and Steve Strange would look like, well... Steve Strange.

Be a SOMEBODY with a BODY

THE PHYSICAL CULTURE SOCIETY

I settled myself in a sumptuous settee in the offices of Limahl's record company, EMI, and tremulously awaited his arrival. Long seconds passed, and then, as is their wont, even longer minutes.

The appointed time drew nearer and my pulse began to race, a cold sweat stood out upon my brow and an electric thrill of highly questionable sexuality tingled through every sinew of my body.

I heard a delicate knock upon the door. The door opened. And there stood (*swoon!*) ... Limahl.

I knew at once that all I had heard about him was true. Meeting him for the first time was one of those rare, unforgettable moments which I shall cherish to my grave. It was like discovering some new and, as yet uncharted territory. All at once I felt as Caesar must have felt when he laid claim to Britain. Yes, this was a case of "I came, I saw, I conquered" — though not necessarily in that order.

Limahl sat opposite me. Well, actually, he sat next to me, on the *same settee*, and after a few initial gasps of adulation from me, the conversation quite naturally got around to a discussion of his body.

"I think the body's a fantastic thing," he said. "And I believe in looking after it. I do sit-ups every night before going to bed. I go swimming twice a week and go to the gym about three times a week to train with weights.

"It's great, because you exercise muscles that you don't normally exercise. Some muscles are very attractive — and that helps with your sex life too!

"I haven't actually built up my muscles much, but I have made them more prominent — just little ones like the muscles in the stomach. The stomach actually has about five different muscular sections, which you can see quite clearly divided in champion weight-lifters. I've got a couple of muscles, here, at the top of my stomach, but it's very difficult to get them further down."

Mopping the perspiration from the palms of my hands, I eagerly questioned Limahl about the various exertions involved in 'Pumping Iron' (as I believe this activity is called in certain circles).

"Actually, I don't normally lift the really heavy weights when I train," he told me, "Because I only weigh eight stone myself! And it can be very embarassing to try to pick up a weight and not be able to do it. Besides, I believe in always starting small and working your way up."

In fact, it appears that this is the philosophy which has shaped not only Limahl's body but also his

LEARN HOW

THE OLIPHANT ACADEMY OF PHYSICAL CULTURE

MUSCLES

FREE INFORMATION

UNIVERSAL BODYBUILDING

career to date. His first public performances were given in the smallest venues you could possibly imagine — well, alright, *almost* the smallest you could imagine...

"I used to sing in local shops," he says. "I'd either sing things from 'The Sound of Music', or current pop songs, and the shop-keepers would give me 10p for it. I was about nine when I first sang in a shop and I carried on doing it till I was about twelve. I've never been nervous of performing in public, even at that age. I was always a cocky little bugger.

"Then, when I was about fifteen, I won a singing contest at the Wigan Casino Club and was presented with fifteen albums by Andy Peebles."

Since then, Limahl has trod the boards in productions ranging from 'Godspell' and Agatha Christie's 'Murder at the Vicarage' to the pantomime, 'Aladdin'.

"That pantomime was my first big break," he recalls. "It was at the Grand Theatre, Swansea, which holds about five hundred people, though sometimes we'd come on for a Monday matinee and find only a hundred people out front. That helped to teach me a lot about how to deal with unresponsive audiences.

"These days, when Kajagoogoo do a live set, I always try to involve the audience as much as possible. I can be very physical when I perform."

Erotic even? I ventured.

"No ... No, No! No!" Limahl rebuked me, "Just physical."

Limahl says that one of his favourite performers is the highly physical and unquestionably erotic Grace Jones, and it seems that it was Ms Jones who, indirectly inspired his own striking two-tone Dulux-dog hair-do.

"I remember being very much impressed by her image and so I went out to try to create an image for myself. Originally, I had my hair done all white, then I put a black streak on one side, then later I added another bit on the other side, then a bit behind, and so on. It progressed, you could say."

And so, the image is now complete — someone for the 'serious' music papers to massacre, the teeny mags to centre-spread and 'Flexipop' to write this sort of drivel about.

But the question remains — is there more to Limahl than just a calculated pose, desirably rippling tummy muscles and increasing bank balance?

Oh, sod-it-all, who the hell cares? You see (*sigh* ...) I think I love him. (*Huw?!? — Ed.*)

CRUSHER KIT★

ONLY WEIGHTS really Work!

AMERICAN HEALTH PRODUCTS LTD 209-211 Longford Rd Coventry

YOU, TOO, CAN HAVE A BODY LIKE MINE!

FREE BOOKLET

I was a 7-stone weakling until I discovered 'Dynamic Tension' the secret method of developing REAL MEN. Send for my free book & details of my 7-day FREE trial offer.

CHARLES ATLAS

Chitty Street, London W1

I heard a delicate knock upon the door. The door opened. And there stood (swoon!)...*Limahl.*

I knew at once that all I had heard about him was true. Meeting him for the first time was one of those rare, unforgettable moments which I shall cherish to my grave. It was like discovering some new and, as yet uncharted territory. All at once I felt as Caesar must have felt when he laid claim to Britain. Yes, this was a case if "I came, I saw, I conquered" - though not necessarily in that order.

Limahl sat opposite me. Well, actually he sat next to me, on the same settee, and after a few initial gasps of adulation from me, the conversation quite naturally got around to a discussion of his body.

"I think the body's a fantastic thing", he said. "And I believe in looking after it. I do sit-ups every night before I go to bed, I go swimming twice a week and go to the gym about three times a week to train with weights.

"It's great, because you exercise muscles that you don't normally exercise. Some muscles are very attractive - and that helps with your sex life too!

"I haven't actually built up my muscles much, but I have made them more prominent - just little ones like the muscles in the stomach. The stomach actually has about five different muscular sections, which you can see quite clearly divided in champion weight-lifters. I've got a couple of muscles, here, at the top of my stomach, but it's very difficult to get them further down".

Mopping the perspiration from the palms of my hands, I eagerly questioned Limahl about the various exertions involved in 'Pumping Iron' (as I believe this activity is called in certain circles).

"Actually, I don't normally lift the really heavy weights when I train," he told me, "Because I only weigh eight stone myself! And it can be very embarrassing to try to pick up a weight and not be able to do it... Besides, I believe in always starting small and working your way up."

In fact, it appears that this is the philosophy which has shaped not only Limahl's body but also his career to date. His first public performances were given in the smallest venues you could possibly imagine - well, alright, almost the smallest you could imagine...

"I used to sing in local shops", he says, "I'd either sing things from *The Sound of Music*, or current pop songs, and the shop-keepers would give me 10p for it.

“I was about nine when I first sang in a shop and carried on doing it till I was about twelve. I've never been nervous of performing in public, even at that age. I was always a cocky little bugger.

"Then, when I was about fifteen, I won a singing contest at the Wigan Casino Club and was presented with fifteen albums by Andy Peebles".

Since then, Limahl has trod the boards in productions ranging from 'Godspell' and Agatha Christie's 'Murder at the Vicarage' to the pantomime, 'Aladdin'.

"That pantomime was my first big break", he recalls, "It was at the Grand Theatre, Swansea, which holds about five hundred people, though sometimes we'd come on for a Monday matinee and find only a hundred people out front. That helped to teach me a lot about how to deal with unresponsive audiences.

"These days, when Kajagoogoo do a live set, I always try to involve the audience as much as possible. I can be very physical when I perform".

Erotic even? I ventured. "No...No, No! No!" Limahl rebuked me, "Just physical".

Limahl says that one of his favourite performers is the highly erotic Grace Jones, and it seems that it was Ms Jones who, indirectly inspired his own striking two-tone Dulux-dog hair-do.

"I remember being very much impressed by her image and so went out to try and create an image for myself. Originally, I had my hair done all white, then I put a black streak on one side, then later I added another bit on the other side, then a bit behind, and so on. It progressed, you could say".

And so, the image is now complete - someone for the 'serious' music papers to massacre, the teeny mags to centre-spread and 'Flexipop' to write this sort of drivel about.

But the question remains - is there more to Limahl than just a calculated pose, desirably rippling tummy muscles and an increasing bank balance?

Oh, sod it all, who the hell cares? You see (sigh...) I think I love him.

(Huw?!? --- Ed.)

LIFELINES

LIMAHL

Real Name: *Chris Hamill*

Date of Birth: *19th, December 1958*

Place of Birth: *Wigan*

Nickname: *The band sometimes calls me 'Limont' because that's what Steve's mother always calls me.*

Previous Jobs: *Hairdresser, barman, shop assistant.*

Most revolting personal habit: *Well, I have been known to pick my nose*

Favourite underwear: *Marks and Spencer.*

Who would you like to throw a custard pie at? *Joan Collins. She always looks so great. It would be nice to see her looking a mess for a change.*

What is the most insulting thing that's ever been written about you?

It was written by Helen Fitzgerald. She said something to the effect that writing the lyrics to 'Ooh To Be Ah' must have really drained my brain.

What do you like wasting money on? *I used to gamble at casinos. I lost a few hundred pounds in just a few weeks. Then I stopped because I could see how silly it was.*

What will you be doing when you are 65? *I hope I'll be long retired.*

If you could be somebody else, who would it be? *Grace Jones.*

If you could be in a film with another pop star, what would the film be and who would be the star? *I'd love to be in a film set in the 1920s or '30s, all about the seedy nightclubs and jazz bars of New York. The group that I'd want to feature in it would be The Manhattan Transfer.*

Most outrageous fantasy: *I bet nobody answers this question truthfully, and I'm going to be no exception! However, one of my most outrageous fantasies is the Queen sitting on the loo. Well, she does, you know. After all, she's only human, like the rest of us...*

Fashion

Don't get the idea that everyone wore kilts and 'pirate shirts'! Early '80s fashion came in a huge range of styles. There were the post-punks and the new wave punks, the Goths, the rockabilly rebels, the head bangers (remember that Heavy Metal was at its height with the likes of Motorhead, Judas Priest, Ozzy and Iron Maiden).

STRANGE WAYS

Steve Strange's connections with clubs go back a long way — Kilt, Blitz, Club for Heroes, and The Camden Palace, to name but a few. His new stomping ground for arbiters of style is The Playground, which is run from London's Lyceum every Saturday.

In fact, Steve has been asked to present a series about Style for Central TV. We thought this was as good a reason as any to invite the man who is described as an inspirational poseur by his friends and a fashion victim by his enemies, to rustle up a few glad rags for Etcetra.

ETC. FASHION

Red leather top hat from Big Apple, 130 Acre Lane, Brixton, £80. Black velvet frock-coat, £500; red waistcoat, £290; black jodhpurs with red stripe, £155, all from Jean Paul Gaultier.

But the there is one style above all others that people associate with those times; it was a style that emerged the clubs of London, Manchester and Birmingham. At first, like an explosion of frilly-shirts and makeup, it was a decidedly theatrical style: resurrected cast-offs from swashbuckling movies of the 1930s with Adam Ant playing the Errol Flynn part and Spandau Ballet, all be-feathered and kilted, looking like bit-part players from some Scottish adventure - Kidnapped maybe, or Rob Roy?

Mixing Goth chic with New Romantic theatricality, Sal Solo and Classix Nouveaux honed the early

who not only looked the part but even used the term 'New Romantic' in their first hit single, 'Planet Earth'...

"Some new romantic looking for the TV sound..."

Toyah meanwhile, having moved on from her punk roots, embraced the new glam vogue with relish and transformed herself into a pixie warrior princess. Seedier under-currents emerged when Soft Cell hit the scene. At first sight they looked like an '80s update to Sparks - with a black-leather and studs makeover. Their groundbreaking album, 'Non-Stop Erotic Cabaret' was released in 1981 and its 'sexual outlaw' theme was to be taken up again, to even greater effect when, in 1984, Frankie Goes

New Romantic style to perfection. Looking back at pictures of Classix Nouveaux now, they seem to sum up the era perfectly. At the time, however, Solo's threatening appearance and the band's hard-hitting music failed to bring them success to rival fellow New Romantics, Duran Duran,

From Steve Strange (left) to Adam Ant (top) - not forgetting Boy George who (above left) showed how men could , with a bit of makeup, transform themselves (as above right)...

To Hollywood released *Relax*, had the single banned by the BBC and become an overnight sensation.

There was another, far less outrageous, side to the fashion of the times. Fashion-leaders such as Steve Strange and Spandau Ballet started moving away from the flamboyant and theatrical and adopting, instead, more sedate styles that recalled an earlier age. Now they favoured tailored jackets, double-breasted suits and even, on occasion, 'country gentleman' tweeds. An exaggerated version of those styles was simultaneously being unleashed in America by a certain Kid Creole. With his Zoot suits, Kid Creole set the standards in a sort of 'cool from the wrong side of the tracks'. Here in the UK bands such as Blue Rondo a la Turk and Matt Bianco were also championing a jazzy, laid-back style that conjured up smoke filled nightclubs and long-legged dames....

In short, there really was no single "style of the times". There were, on the contrary, a great many of them...

THE WINTER COLLECTION

NEW MASTERS have a really stunning range of wear in their Winter Collection. Here we see Buster in one of the highlights of the Anne Smith Folie. Dressed in matching jumper (£23), skirt (£21) and socks (£6.50), I think that any man could be guaranteed to get quite a few admiring glances. Anne Smith has taken something of a pioneering approach in this outfit. Features to note at the 'open gusset' which not only ensures a feeling of freedom to the wearer, but can also be adapted, by tying the cords between the legs, into a 'short-trouser' look. In fact, it provides something for all occasions.

HERE WE see Buster modelling a fetching little ensemble from WORLD'S END. Beneath a sheepskin overcoat in saip at (£290), he has a pullover in a complementing colour (£40), a pair of figure-hugging trousers, (£35) and over-leggings (£12). The mood here is redolent of Autumn, and as you can see, Buster cuts quite a dash in this striking outfit. The whole effect is, of course, brilliantly set-off by the matching hat, which is a speciality of this House, costing a mere £25.

IT IS at this time of the year that all the leading couturiers are preparing their Winter Collections - clothes whose exclusive fabrics and fashions will soon be seen gracing the élite of the haut-monde at balls, parties and premieres during the coming Season.

With the new wave of young designers, fashion is no longer hide-bound by the conventions set by such past masters as Saint-Laurent and Hartnell. There is a new and vigorous spirit pervading the modern movement. Nowadays style is not the exclusive preserve of the sylph-like mannequins of yesteryear; indeed, one of the exciting trends which we have observed in recent times is the movement towards really inventive fashions for the "fuller" man. We took one of the leading exponents of the so-called "Nouvelle Grosseur", Buster Bloodvessel, to try on a few of the latest creations of some of the leading Fashion Houses in the King's Road, at the very heart of elegant Chelsea . . .

Even Buster Bloodvessel was putting on the style - with, one would have to say, somewhat limited success...

Things I Wish I'd Known At 15

My head was full of a load of junk when I was fifteen. I knew I wanted to be a pop star but I didn't know how to go about it and I really had no idca of what to expect of the pop world.

I hated school and I left it when I was fifteen and went to an engineering college for six months until I got myself an engineering apprenticeship which lasted for two and a half years.

What I really wanted to do was to get out of Glasgow and move down to London. To make a name in the music business you have to come to London at some time. Glasgow seemed like a complete musical desert to me. There was nowhere for a band to play, no rehearsal rooms and no recording studios. The town just wasn't geared to bands at all, though the situation has improved a lot now.

I didn't have the confidence in myself to chuck in my job, uproot myself completely and come down to London. With hindsight, I have to say I'm glad I didn't - moving down to London at that age would have been a really bad thing for me. I think I could easily have got sucked into the wrong areas and ended up by going back to Glasgow with my tail between my legs. In the end, I didn't move to London until I was twenty-three and big enough to cope with whatever came at me.

At fifteen I definitely had illusions of grandeur. I suppose I thought of myself as a star just waiting to be discovered. It took years for me to discover that it wasn't like that at all. It's been hard work to get where I am today and I've made a lot of bad mistakes along the way. But would it have been any easier for me it if I'd known at the age of fifteen the things that I know now? I'm not sure. I don't think it would, because, unfortunately, the only way you can really learn anything is by experience.

If I'd done anything different - if, for example, I had moved to London earlier - maybe I wouldn't be doing what I am now. I might not have been able to make it as a musician in London at that age.

I think the length of time I stayed in Glasgow may have helped me. All the time I was working as an apprentice I was also serving my 'musical apprenticeship' by playing in a local band at weekends.

My first 'break' came when a friend of mine went along to audition as keyboard player with a full-time group. I went along with him and while he did his audition, the band asked me if I'd fill in by playing some guitar. As a result, my friend didn't get the job, but I did!

I had to give up my engineering apprenticeship to join the band. The people at work couldn't believe it when I told them that I was throwing in a good job to go and become a musician. One thing I do wish I'd known at fifteen is that you shouldn't believe what people tell you. And that applies just as much when people say complimentary things as when they criticise you.

Even when I was seventeen or eighteen I still used to believe it when people would say 'Wow, what a guitar player! What a star!' So when I joined Slik and we had a successful record I thought: 'Hey, they are right, I *am* a star!' and so I started behaving the way I thought a star should behave - in other words, like a prat.

Then, six months later, when all that was whipped from under my feet, I couldn't take it. Some musicians go to pieces when they no longer get all that adulation or have people asking them to do interviews. Luckily, I did manage to pull myself together, but it was quite a shock to my ego.

Another thing I wish I'd known was that you have to be pretty hard-headed in a business sense to get anywhere. It's no good singing and playing your guitar while spending lots of money and leaving somebody else to worry about that.

My business associates in the early years were as naive as I was. We went through some really dodgy patches and ended up owing fortunes to our management. Every time we flew from Glasgow to London to do TV or a photosession they'd pay for it. When Slik ended we owed £100,000 to these people. That's a hell of a lot to owe someone when you're twenty

That experience made me very wary of people and I didn't trust anyone for six months after the Slik fiasco. I didn't realise how important the business side of pop was. I just loved the ides of being a pop star going out in front of people who actually wanted to see and hear you. In fact, it wasn't until about three years ago that that actually happened. Before that I'd just been with bands who played in corners like some human juke-box occasionally being spat at or having bottles thrown at us. I'd like to have arrived at the sort of success that I have with Ultravox when I was about eighteen. Then the last ten years would have been really fun. But then, who knows, if that had happened, maybe I would have burnt myself out by the time I got to twenty-two?... So perhaps things turned out for the best after all...

EUROPE AFTER THE RAIN...

In 1981, John Foxx, formerly the lead singer with Ultravox, released a single called '*Europe After The Rain*'. It summed up a good deal of the mood, the style and the atmosphere that lay behind much of the musical and fashion movement loosely known as New Romanticism.That same year, Foxx's old band released *Vienna* - one of the most memorable songs of the period which, along with its video, self-consciously conjured up the strangely romantic yet threatening ambiance of post-war Europe that was crystallized in the 1949 movie, *The Third Man*. Midge Ure, who was by now the Ultravox singer, was also one of the main forces behind the ultimate New Romantic group, Visage. Once again the songs - for example, *Night Train* and *The Damned Don't Cry* - are redolent of the atmosphere of 'old Europe' as transmitted through the lens of old Hollywood. Even the group's name, Visage, is French, as are some lyrics of their most famous song, *Fade To Grey*. French (or pseudo-French) names were clearly pretty cool at that time. Think of Classix Nouveaux (whose lead-singer, Sal Solo, is pictured below), not to mention Depeche Mode and Cabaret Voltaire. The influence of the film, *Cabaret*, shouldn't be underestimated either. This was most clearly seen in the song, *Drowning In Berlin* by The Mobiles. But its influence, both in terms of music and - even more of imagery ('divine decadence, darling'), was widespread...

David Sylvian

REPUGNANT HUW COLLINGBOURNE TALKS TO GORGEOUS, BEAUTIFUL **DAVID SYLVIAN** OF JAPAN

HOW OFTEN had I gasped at the whispered rumours of his unearthly beauty! How many sleepless nights had I tearfully passed, assailed by secret tremblings of envy at the very thought of his enthralling loveliness!

It is said that in lands of distant Orient he is worshipped as a god. Words cannot express the torment of inferiority suffered by all men in contemplation radiant fairness of David Sylvian's sublime good looks. So, when at last we met, my heart was a-flutter. Here was I, an ordinary lad with greasy hair, and there was he . . . at twenty-three the very flower of masculine splendour.

What, I wondered, was the secret of his unparalleled comeliness?

"I am not very attractive," he said firmly as the sunlight glimmered on his perfect skin, "In fact I feel quite the opposite. But I know my faults and if you know your faults you can make the best of what you are."

You mean that, with a little help, too could aspire to such exquisiteness? Oh, David, tell me how!

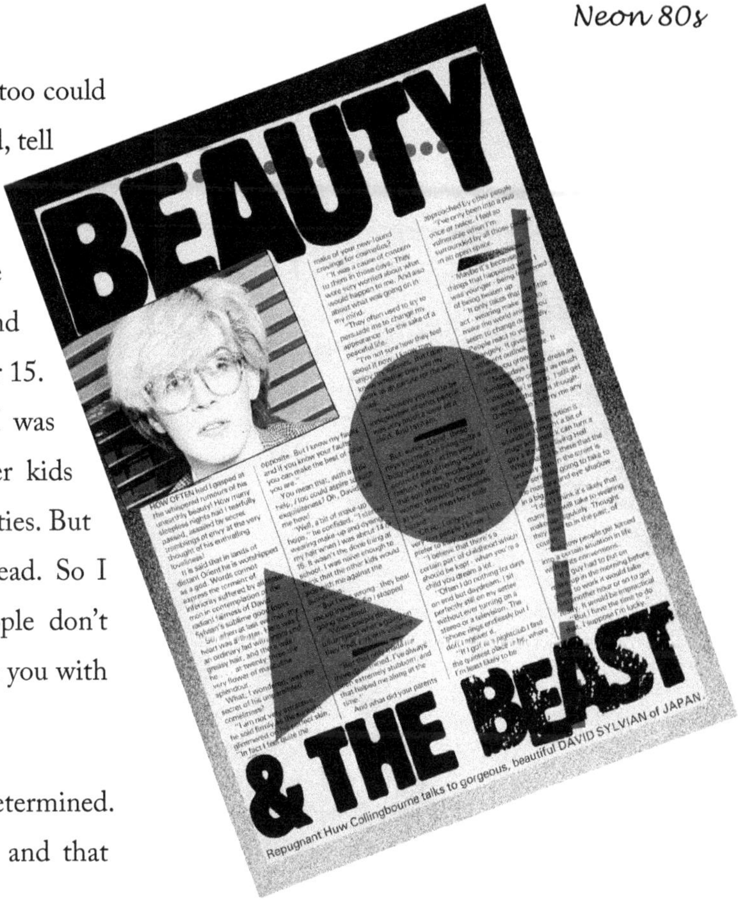

"Well, a bit of makeup helps," he confided, "I started wearing makeup and dyeing my hair when I was about 14 or 15. It wasn't the done thing at school. I was naive enough to think that the other kids would side with me against the authorities. But I was wrong – they beat me up instead. So I stopped going to school. When people don't understand what's going on, they treat you with violence.

"But that only made me more determined. I've always been extremely stubborn, and that helped me along at the time."

"It only takes that one little act - wearing makeup make – to make the world around you seem to change drastically"

And what did your parents make of your new-found cravings for cosmetics?

"It was a cause of concern to them in those days. They were very worried about what would happen to me. And also about what was going on in my mind. They often used to try to persuade me to change my appearance - for the sake of a peaceful life.

"I'm not sure how they feel about it now. I know they enjoy my success. But I don't know whether they use my work as an excuse for the way I look.

"I've always yearned to be independent of other people. I was very much a loner as a child. And I still am."

But surely, David, these days you must be living quite a busy social life – at the very centre of the glittering world of fashion, parties, models and all that sort of thing? Gorgeous women throwing themselves at your feet must be a daily hazard.

"Oh no. I only mix with the very few people I know. I prefer to stay indoors.

space. Maybe it's because of things that happened when was younger - being frightened of being beaten up.

"It only takes that one little act - wearing makeup – to make the world around you seem to change drastically. People react to you so strangely. It gives you a different outlook on life. It makes you grow up.

"Nowadays I don't dress up as flamboyantly or wear as much makeup as I used to. I still get remarks on the street, though. Only it doesn't worry me any more."

From this description it sounds as though a bit of rouge and lipstick can turn a guy's life into a living Hell. What chance is there that the ordinary man in the street is ever seriously going to take to the mascara and eye-shadow in a big way?

"I believe that there's a certain part of childhood which should be kept - when you're a child you dream a lot. Often I do nothing for days on end but daydream. I sit perfectly still on my settee without ever turning on a stereo or a television. The 'phone rings endlessly but I don't answer it. If I go to a nightclub I find the quietest place to be, where I'm least likely to be approached by other people. I've only been into a pub once or twice. I feel so vulnerable when I'm surrounded by all those people in an open

"I don't think it's likely that many men will take to wearing makeup regularly. Though they used to in the past, of course.

"But now people get forced a certain situation in life with all its conventions.

"If a guy had to put on makeup in the morning before to work it would take another hour or so to get ready. It would be impractical. "But I have the time to do that.. I suppose I'm lucky."

Adam Ant

Dandy Highwayman...

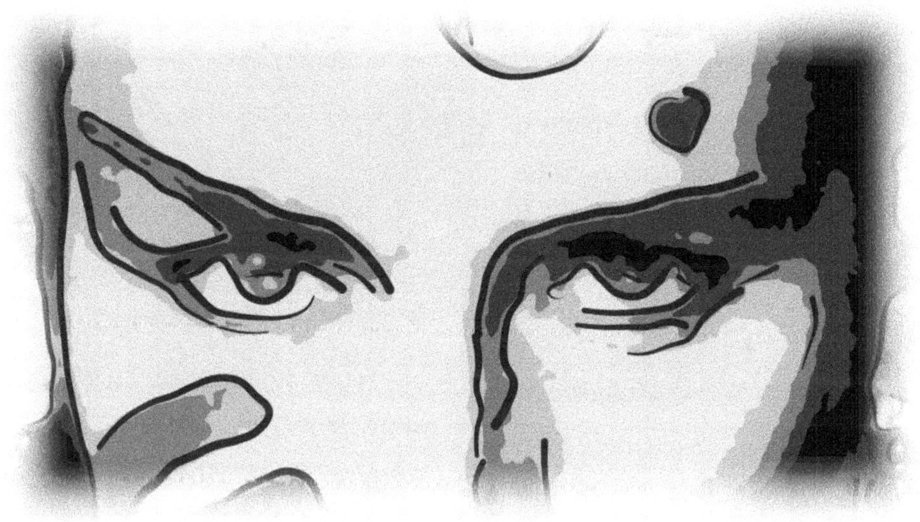

A couple of years ago, Adam Ant was, without any doubt, the biggest name in top. With a string of hit records to his name, such as 'Ant Music', 'Kings Of The 'Wild Frontier', 'Stand and Deliver' and 'Prince Charming' it seemed that he just couldn't fail. And then he surprised everyone when he and the Ants decided to go their separate ways. Adam's way led him to America where he has spent the last two years touring, trying to establish himself as a solo artist.

Now he has returned to Britain for good. But can he seriously hope to regain his domination of the charts? After all, a lot has happened since he's been away - Duran Duran, Frankie and Boy George to name but a few.

Adam's got a tough job ahead of him. But when we met him recently, he was far from downhearted...

You've changed your image quite a lot since the 'highwayman' look. Why is that?

I think it's a big danger in pop music to try to play safe and stick with the image that you start with. There's the risk that you'll be stuck with it for ever like Alice Cooper or Gary Glitter.

But aren't you stuck with your old look anyway? People still think of 'Stand and Deliver' image as the real Adam Ant.

Up to a point, I think that's true. You have to get used to the idea that the image that you start out with is the one that will stick with you for the rest of your life. Even now

The Beatles are still associated with those four cheeky chappies in suits - and people still remember Bowie as Ziggy Stardust. And yes, a lot of people do still think of me as the 'highwayman'. That doesn't bother me. I accept it as a compliment. It was the look that made people take notice of me. I'll never go back to it, though. Although I feel now that I am going back to those early days in a different way - through the excitement of the music.

You've been through so many 'looks' since you started that it's beginning to get difficult to remember what you actually look like.

With the benefit of hindsight I'd have to admit that I did go from the 'warrior look' to the highwayman to Prince Charming much too fast and then I changed again for my solo career. It was all much too drastic. I'm going to take more time in future, though

What do you think of the way that Boy George has changed his image?

I don't think that his new look is particularly different from his old look. He's undone the locks and taken the hat off. Apart from that, there's no change.

Do you approve of the fashion for men to wear makeup?

I think men should use makeup to enhance their features. But the emphasis is all on 'pretty boys' at the moment. It all seems a bit safe. There's not a lot of 'oomph' there.

What style of clothes do you go in for during your everyday life these days?

I have most of my clothes specially made. Even my shirts are made to my own specifications. That way I can choose exactly the colour, pattern and fit that I want. It's nice to have things made by a craftsman.

Unfortunately, really good style doesn't come cheap. I've always bought fairly expensive clothes. Even when I was a teenager doing a weekend job, I used to go to a shop called 'Sex' in the King's Road where the clothes were very dear. I'd pay maybe £35 for a pair of suede boots. I could hardly afford them but they were worth it in the end. I'm wearing one of those old pairs of boots at the moment - and they still look good! I suppose, having had a training in art, I tend to be more critical of the look of things then many people.

Do you still do any of your own art work?

I design my costumes and record covers and I draw out the storyboards for my videos. But I don't have the time to do full-scale paintings.

You were one of the first pop stars really to exploit video. What's your opinion of all the pop videos which have been made since then?

I'm not impressed. Most of them have no imagination. They just have cars, beaches and girls. Over the past four years I've made ten videos and I think I can understand their worth. It's a pity that so many people don't seem to know what to do with them.

You've worked with Marco ever since the early days yet he always seems to get left in the background. Doesn't he resent the way that you always hog the limelight?

Marco does step into the limelight too from time to time when we perform but on the whole he seems to prefer the shadows. He's very different from me. We're like chalk and cheese, in fact. He's very quiet and I'm very talkative. We don't like the same type of food or the same style of living. He comes alive at night and I prefer to work in the day. I stick up front and he stays in the background.

Do you think the split from the Ants was a mistake?

No. I'll tell, you what my biggest mistake was though. It was when I signed with an independent record company in 1978. I thought they were going to be The Great Alternative, but really they were just as greedy as everybody else.

Recently you've had a few offers of parts in feature films such as 'Nomads'. Do you think you'll give up pop music to concentrate on this side of your career?

I'll never do that. I'll never grow sick of Pop music. It's so exciting to me. The funny thing is, even when I get offered parts in films, you go along to read the script and the Director turns to you and says, 'Oh, by the way, Adam, I thought it might be a good idea if you sang a song just here...' It seems that I couldn't get away from music even if I wanted to!

Adam Ant

The Naked Truth...

Earlier this year you were voted The sexiest Man of 1984 by the American magazine, 'Rock'. What did you do to deserve such a title?

I'm not sure. I was surprised as anyone else by that. Previous winners have been people like Sting, Bowie and Simon Le Bon. It's a very strange feeling to have people voting about your sexiness. Of course, the Americans did see the 'Strip' video and show which weren't seen in Britain, so maybe that helped. I'm waiting for my prize to arrive now.

Why did we never get to see the 'Strip' video and show?

The BBC banned the video of 'Strip'. I had intended to tour with the show, but after the video was banned, my plans went out the window.

What was so shocking about the video?

Nothing. I'm still mystified as to all the fuss it caused. They said that I was doing certain things in the video which I certainly wasn't. I never intended it to be sensational.

When 'Relax' was banned, it seemed to do nothing but good for Frankie Goes To Hollywood. Why didn't the controversy about your video help you in the same way?

'Relax' was a freak situation. It's the first time something like that has happened since The Sex Pistols caused a lot of fuss when they appeared on Bill Grundy's TV show. Bill Grundy made The Sex Pistols successful and I think Mike Read will. go down in history as making Frankie Goes To Hollywood successful. But controversy works against me because my success has never been based on controversy. I was very shocked by the ban.

If there was nothing shocking in your video, why did the BBC object?

The reason I was given was that I'd forgotten who my audience was. That puzzled me because I have no age-limit on my records. My work has always had a very sexual nature. I have never made bubblegum, teenybop records in my life, Adam and the Ants were playing in punk clubs for years before we had any commercial success.

When I went on to do things like The Royal Variety Performance and the Cannon and Ball Show, people misinterpreted that and thought I was trying to be a 'family entertainer.' I just did it because it seemed more fun than doing the very serious music programmes.

It's fairly well known that you don't smoke or drink, and you don't go out to clubs much either. What do you do for fun these days?

There are two basic luxuries in my life. One is getting cabs everywhere because I don't drive. And the other is eating out.

I go to lots of nice, private restaurants where I'm sure I won't be seen and know there won't be any Press there. The waiters all know me and they know that I'm not going to do anything silly like come in with a guitar and start blasting the walls down. They almost protect me from other people, which is nice.

In some ways you seem to have a very Puritanical approach to life. You've never been a part of the hard living hard drinking brigade. You're anti-drinking, anti-drugs and you say you like to keep regular hours. You almost sound like a modern version of Cliff Richard - if it wasn't for all the sexual overtones.

I don't see why I should ruin my body and my life just because I happen to be in pop music. And even though I am a very sexual performer, I don't think I'm dirty.

O.K., so what did go on in the 'Strip' show that we never saw in Britain?

I'd better explain that the whole theme of 'Strip' wasn't what it seemed. 'I was trying to reverse people's expectations of me. I've always been thought of as somebody who dresses up a lot. This time I was going to take things off rather than put them on. I ended up getting into a tank of water on stage. It was very dangerous because of the electricity and the UK safety regulations wouldn't permit it. I did a sort of strip-tease, ending up wearing nothing but leg warmers and shorts. Then I'd throw away the leg warmers.

And the shorts?

Oh no. I can assure you it was all done in the best possible taste!

...SEVEN DAYS WITH POPSTAR, BUNNY LOVER AND TRAINEE ACCOUNTANT

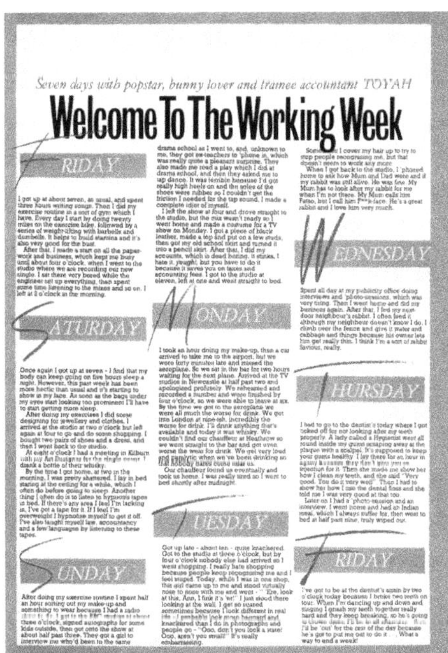

Seven days with popstar, bunny lover and trainee accountant TOYAH

Welcome To The Working Week

FRIDAY

I got up at about seven, as usual, and spent three hours writing songs. Then I did my exercise routine in a sort of gym which I have. Every day I start by doing twenty miles on the exercise bike, followed by a series of weight-lifting with barbells and dumbells. It helps to build stamina and it's also very good for the bust.

After that, I made a start on all the paper-work and business, which kept me busy until about four o'clock, when I went to the studio where we are recording our new single. I sat there very bored while the engineer set up everything, then spent some time listening to the mixes and so on. I left at 2 o'clock in the morning.

SATURDAY

Once again I got up at seven - I find that my body can keep going on five hours sleep a night. However, this past week has been more hectic than usual and it's starting to show in my face. As soon as the bags under my eyes start looking too prominent I'll have to start getting more sleep.

After doing my exercises I did some designing for jewellery and clothes. I arrived at the studio at two o'clock but left again at four to go and do some shopping. I bought two pairs of shoes and a dress, and then I went back to the studio.

At eight o'clock I had a meeting in Kilburn with my Art Designers for the single cover. I drank a bottle of their whisky.

By the time I got home, at two in the morning, I was pretty shattered. I lay in bed staring at the ceiling for a while, which I often do before going to sleep. Another thing I often do is to listen to hypnosis tapes in bed. If there's any area I feel I'm lacking in, I've got a tape for it. If I feel I'm overweight I hypnotise myself to get it off. I've also taught myself law, accountancy and a few languages by listening to these tapes.

SUNDAY

After doing my exercise routine I spent half an hour sorting out my make-up and something to wear because I had a radio [illegible] I got to the BBC studios at about three o'clock, signed autographs for some kids outside, then got onto the show at about half past three. They got a girl to interview me who'd been to the same drama school as I went to, and, unknown to me, they got ex-teachers to 'phone in, which was really quite a pleasant surprise. They also made me read a play which I did at drama school, and then they asked me to tap dance. It was terrible because I'd got really high heels on and the soles of the shoes were rubber so I couldn't get the friction I needed for the tap sound. I made a complete idiot of myself.

I left the show at four and drove straight to the studio, but the mix wasn't ready so I went home and made a costume for a TV show on Monday. I got a piece of black leather, made a top and put on a few studs, then got my old school skirt and turned it into a pencil skirt. After that, I did my accounts, which is dead boring, it stinks, I hate it, *yeugh!*, but you have to do it because it saves you on taxes and accounting fees. I got to the studio at eleven, left at one and went straight to bed.

MONDAY

I took an hour doing my make-up, then a car arrived to take me to the airport, but we were forty minutes late and missed the aeroplane. So we sat in the bar for two hours waiting for the next plane. Arrived at the TV studios in Newcastle at half past two and apologised profusely. We rehearsed and recorded a number and were finished by four o'clock, so we were able to leave at six. By the time we got to the aeroplane we were all much the worse for drink. We got into London at nine-ish, incredibly the worse for drink. I'll drink anything that's available and today it was whisky. We couldn't find our chauffeur at Heathrow so we went straight to the bar and got even worse the wear for drink. We get very loud and [illegible] when we've been drinking so that nobody dares come near us.

Our chauffeur found us eventually and took us home. I was really tired so I went to bed shortly after midnight.

TUESDAY

Got up late - about ten - quite knackered. Got to the studio at three o'clock, but by four o'clock nobody else had arrived so I went shopping. I really hate shopping because people keep recognising me and I feel stupid. Today, while I was in one shop, this girl came up to me and stood virtually nose to nose with me and went - " 'Ere, look at this, Ann, I fink it's 'er!" I just stood there looking at the wall. I get so scared sometimes because I look different in real life - I probably look more haggard and knackered than I do in photographs and people go - "Ooo, don't you look a state! Ooo, aren't you small!" It's really embarrassing.

Sometimes I cover my hair up to try to stop people recognising me, but that doesn't seem to work any more.

When I got back to the studio, I 'phoned home to ask how Mum and Dad were and if my rabbit was still alive. He was fine. My Mum has to look after my rabbit for me when I'm not there. My Mum calls him Fatso, but I call him F**k-face. He's a great rabbit and I love him very much.

WEDNESDAY

Spent all day at my publicity office doing interviews and 'photo-sessions, which was very tiring. Then I went home and did my business again. After that, I fed my next-door neighbour's rabbit. I often feed it although my neighbour doesn't know I do. I climb over the fence and give it water and cabbage and things because his owner lets him get really thin. I think I'm a sort of rabbit Saviour, really.

THURSDAY

I had to go to the dentist's today where I got ticked off for not looking after my teeth properly. A lady called a Hygienist went all round inside my gums scraping away at the plaque with a scalpel. It's supposed to keep your gums healthy. I lay there for an hour in agony [illegible] Then she made me show her how I clean my teeth, and she said "Very good. You do it very well". Then I had to show her how I use the dental floss and she told me I was very good at that too.

Later on I had a 'photo-session and an interview. I went home and had an Indian meal, which I always suffer for, then went to bed at half past nine, truly wiped out.

FRIDAY

I've got to be at the dentist's again by two o'clock today because I broke two teeth on tour. When I'm dancing up and down and singing I gnash my teeth together really hard and they keep breaking, so he's going to [illegible] I'll be 'out' for the rest of the day because he's got to put me out to do it . . . What a way to end a week!

Friday

I got up at about seven, as usual, and spent three hours writing songs. Then I did my exercise routine in a sort of gym which I have. Every day I start by doing twenty miles on the exercise bike, followed by a series of weight-lifting with barbells and dumbbells. It helps to build stamina and it's also very good for the bust. After that, I made a start on all the paperwork and business, which kept me busy until about four o'clock, when I went to the studio where we are recording our new single. I sat there very bored while the engineer set up everything, then spent some time listening to the mixes and so on. I left at 2 o'clock in the morning.

Saturday

Once again I got up at seven - I find that my body can keep going on five hours sleep a night. However, this past week has been more hectic than usual and it's starting to show in my face. As soon as the bags under my eyes start looking too prominent I'll have to start getting more sleep.

After doing my exercises I did some designing for jewellery and clothes. I arrived at the studio at two o'clock but left again at four to go and do some shopping. I bought two pairs of shoes and a dress, and then I went back to the studio. At eight o'clock I had a meeting in Kilburn with my Art Designer for the single cover. I drank a bottle of their whisky.

By the time I got home, at two in the morning, I was pretty shattered. I lay in bed staring at the ceiling for a while, which I often do before going to sleep. Another thing I often do is to listen to hypnosis tapes in bed. If there's any area I feel I'm lacking in, I've got a tape for it. If I feel I'm overweight I hypnotise myself to get it off. I've also taught myself law, accountancy and a few languages by listening to these tapes.

Sunday

After doing my exercise routine I spent half an hour sorting out my makeup and something to wear because I had a radio show to do. I got to the BBC studios at about three o'clock, signed autographs for some kids outside, then got onto the show at about half past three

They got a girl to interview me who'd been to the same drama school as I went to, and, unknown to me, they got ex-teachers to 'phone in, which was really quite a pleasant surprise. They also made me read a play which I did at drama school, and then they asked me to tap dance. It was terrible because I'd got really high heels on and the soles of the shoes were rubber so I couldn't get the friction I needed for the tap sound. I made a complete idiot of myself.

I left the show at four and drove straight to the studio, but the mix wasn't ready so I went home and made a costume for a TV show on Monday. I got a piece of black leather, made a top and put on a few studs, then got my old school skirt and turned it into a pencil skirt. After that, I did my accounts, which is dead boring, it stinks, I hate it, yeugh!, but you have to do it because it saves you on taxes and accounting fees. I got to the studio at eleven, left at one and went straight to bed.

Monday

I took an hour doing my makeup, then a car arrived to take me to the airport, but we were forty minutes late and missed the aeroplane. So we sat in the bar for two hours waiting for the next plane. Arrived at the TV studios in Newcastle at half past two and apologised profusely.

We rehearsed and recorded a number and were finished by four o'clock, so we were able to leave at six. By the time we got to the aeroplane we were all much the worse for drink. We got into London at nine-ish, incredibly the worse for drink. I'll drink anything that's available and today it was whisky. We couldn't find our chauffeur at Heathrow so we went straight to the bar and got even worse the wear for drink. We get very loud and paralytic when we've been drinking so that nobody dares come near us.

Our chauffeur found us eventually and took us home. I was really tired so I went to bed shortly after midnight.

Tuesday

Got up late - about ten - quite knackered. Got to the studio at three o'clock, but by four o'clock nobody else had arrived so I went shopping. I really hate shopping because people keep recognising me and I feel stupid. Today, while I was in one shop, this girl came up to me and stood virtually nose to nose with me and went - "'Ere, look at this, Ann, I fink it's 'er!" I just stood there looking at the wall. I get so scared sometimes because I look different in real life - I probably look more haggard and knackered than I do in photographs and people go - "Ooo, don't you look a state! Ooo aren't you small!" It's really embarrassing.

Sometimes I cover my hair up to try to stop people recognising me, but that doesn't seem to work any more.

When I got to the studio, I 'phoned home to ask how Mum and Dad were and if my rabbit was still alive. He was fine. My Mum has to look after my rabbit for me when I'm not there. My Mum calls him Fatso, but I call him F**k-face. He's a great rabbit and I love him very much.

Wednesday

Spent all day at my publicity office doing interviews and 'photo-sessions, which was very tiring. Then I went home and did my business again. After that, I fed my next-door neighbour's rabbit. I often feed it although my neighbour doesn't know I do. I climb over the fence and give it water and cabbage and things because his owner lets him get really thin. I think I'm a sort of rabbit Saviour, really.

Thursday

I had to go to the dentist's today where I got ticked off for not looking after my teeth properly. A lady called a Hygienist went all round inside my gums scraping away at the plaque with a scalpel. It's supposed to keep your gums healthy. I lay there for an hour in agony because they don't give you an injection for it. Then she made me show her how I clean my teeth, and she said "Very good. You do it very well". Then I had to show her how I use the dental floss and she told me I was very good at that too. Later on I had a 'photo-session and an interview. I went home and had an Indian meal, which I always suffer for, then went to bed at half past nine, truly wiped out.

Friday

I've got to be at the dentist's again by two o'clock today because I broke two teeth on tour. When I'm dancing up and down and singing I gnash my teeth together really hard and they keep breaking, so he's going to crown them. I'll be in all afternoon - then I'll be `out' for the rest of the day because he's got to put me out to do it . . . What a way to end a week!

Modern Romance

Geoffrey & David pout for slim-hipped Huw Collingbourne

The air is hot and oppressive. Outside the window the streets of Soho swelter in the sultry heat. As I undo another shirt button I can feel little rivulets of sweat trickling down over my body towards dark and uncharted territories.

By contrast, the four elegant youths opposite me are as cool as the chilled white wine which they delicately sip. I decide to keep the tempo way down - I don't feel in the mood to shake it in the Latin groove. And none of my grooves are in any fit state to have things shaken in them anyway.

I'm racking my brains for some off-beat, probing question to ask these guys - but they look too nice to have any guilty secrets. In desperation I steer the easy course.

MODERN ROMANCE. . . with a name like that just how romantic are they? Geoffrey Deane elegantly uncrosses his legs. He looks across at David Jaymes whose golden blond hair shimmers in the rays of the sun filtering through the Venetian blinds -"We love each other," he says tenderly.

My heart misses a beat. But then I glance again at Geoffrey. Is he being on-the level? Or is he just making the kind of deliberately provocative statement that he thinks I'll never dare repeat in print? David Jaymes, meanwhile, is saying nothing on the matter. Wearing a powder blue suit and an air of cultivated gentility, all he wants to talk about is Style:

"It's how you carry it off. It's the way that you walk. It's the way you do everything. It's the way I'm gesticulating now with my cigarette," he says, gesticulating stylishly with his cigarette.

"Whatever Spandau Ballet haven't got - that's what it is!" Geoffrey adds in his rather more forthright manner.

"Although, wearing pink suits can cause problems," David admits.

"The further North you go the harder it gets," Geoffrey explains, "Because anyone who hasn't got a broken jaw is invariably homosexual as far as they are concerned. And there's always one person who'll get jealous because his girlfriend has looked twice at one of the group."

David Jaymes

Jealous? But wait a minute . . . if they think you're all gay . . .?

"Well, they all think we're very effeminate, lets put it that way," breaks in duskily good-looking Andy Kyriacou.

Not that these lads are bothered by what anybody thinks of them - or so they insist.

The people they admire most (apart from one another, that is) are "people with cavalier attitudes - people who will stand out on a limb and say what might be regarded as outrageous things."

Their heroes make a fairly improbable bunch, including Oscar Wilde, Brian Clough and Trevor Howard because when he's on chat shows "he's always outrageously drunk and makes caustic comments."

David and Geoffrey have spent ten happy and productive years together. Isn't that a little bit like being married to one another? Andy pipes up again in answer to that - "Put it this way - they get jealous if either of them goes out with somebody without the other one!"

"In many ways," says Geoff, "at the risk of incriminating ourselves it is like a marriage. We are very firm friends. I think, personally, there is something about male/male friendships that is substantially different from female to female friendships."

And what about them quaint, old-fashioned male/female relationships?

"Oh, we've split up with hosts of girlfriends," Geoff says.

Why all the splitting up? Nothing to do with David and Geoffs' 'Very Special Friendship,' perchance.

"It has caused tensions and problems in the past," David admits cautiously, "but fortunately we've got two very understanding girlfriends . . .

Sigh . .I can't help it but I really do think all this is ever so heart-warming. Like Courtly Brotherhood and all that - you know, the stuff all those dashing knights of yore went in for in a big way. All that derring-do for dusky maidens one minute - and then off back home to one another the next.

Just as I'm beginning to gurgle sentimentally into my Coca-Cola, Geoff jolts me back to modern reality and tarnishes my dream of Chivalrous Romance just the teensiest bit...

"We always try and make sure that we have at least one night a week when we go out and get blind drunk and meet anyone and when they ask us what we are we say we're bus drivers or something . . .

Bus drivers? Why bus drivers?

Somehow I just can't bring myself to imagine Sir Galahad trying that one on with the local damsels.

THE even ODDER couple

GEOFFREY & DAVID pout for slim-hipped Huw Collingbourne

THE AIR is hot and oppressive. Outside the window the streets of Soho swelter in the sultry heat. As I undo another shirt button I can feel little rivulets of sweat trickling down over my body towards dark and uncharted territories.

By contrast, the four elegant youths opposite me are as cool as the chilled white wine which they delicately sip. I decide to keep the tempo way down - I don't feel in the mood to shake it in the latin groove. And none of my grooves are in any fit state to have things shaken in them anyway.

I'm racking my brains for some off-beat, probing question to ask these guys - but they look too nice to have any guilty secrets. In desperation I steer the easy course.

MODERN ROMANCE

. . . with a name like that just how romantic are they?

Geoffrey Deane elegantly uncrosses his legs. He looks across at David Jaymes whose golden blond hair shimmers in the rays of the sun filtering through the Venetian blinds. "We love each other," he says tenderly.

My heart misses a beat.

But then I glance again at Geoffrey. Is he being on-the-level? Or is he just making the kind of deliberately provocative statement that he thinks I'll never dare repeat in print?

David Jaymes, meanwhile, is saying nothing on the matter. Wearing a powder blue suit and an air of cultivated gentility, all he wants to talk about is Style.

"It's how you carry it off. It's the way that you walk. It's the way you do everything. It's the way I'm gesticulating now with my cigarette," he says, gesticulating stylishly with his cigarette.

"Whatever Spandau Ballet haven't got - that's what it is!" Geoffrey adds in his rather more forthright manner.

"Although, wearing pink suits can cause problems," David admits.

"The further North you go the harder it gets," Geoffrey explains. "Because anyone who hasn't got a broken jaw is invariably homosexual as far as they are concerned."

"And there's always one person who'll get jealous because his girlfriend has looked twice at one of the group."

Jealous? But wait a minute . . . if they think you're all gay . . . ?

"Well, they all think we're very *effeminate*, lets put it that way," breaks in duskily good-looking Andy Kyriacou.

Not that these lads are bothered by what anybody thinks of them - or so they insist.

The people they admire most (apart from one another, that is) are "people with cavalier attitudes - people who will stand out on a limb and say what might be regarded as outrageous things."

Their heroes make a fairly improbable bunch, including Oscar Wilde, Brian Clough and Trevor Howard because when he's on chat shows "he's always outrageously drunk and makes caustic comments."

David and Geoffrey have spent ten happy and productive years together.

Isn't that a little bit like being married to one another?

Andy pipes up again in answer to that: "Put it this way - they get jealous if either of them goes out with somebody without the other one!"

"In many ways," says Geoff, "at the risk of incriminating ourselves it is like a marriage. We are very firm friends.

"I think, personally, there is something about male/male friendships that is substantially different from female to female friendships."

And what about them quaint, old-fashioned male/female relationships?

"Oh, we've split up with hosts of girlfriends," Geoff says.

Why all the splitting up? Nothing to do with David and Geoffs' 'Very Special Friendship,' perchance.

"It has caused tensions and problems in the past," David admits cautiously, "but fortunately we've got two very understanding girlfriends . . ."

Sigh . . . I can't help it but I really do think all this is ever so heartwarming. Like Courtly Brotherhood and all that - you know, the stuff all those dashing knights of yore went in for in a big way. All that derring-do for dusky maidens one minute - and then off back home to *one another* the next.

Just as I'm beginning to gurgle sentimentally into my CocaCola, Geoff jolts me back to modern reality and tarnishes my dream of Chivalrous Romance just the teensiest bit . . .

"We always try and make sure that we have at least one night a week when we go out and get blind drunk and meet anyone and when they ask us what we are we say we're bus drivers or something . . ."

Bus drivers? Why bus drivers?

Somehow I just can't bring myself to imagine Sir Galahad trying *that* one on with the **local damsels.**

Pic: Simon Fowler

I met David Jaymes several times and got on well with him. Nice of him to forgive this interview, really... ;-)

Matt Bianco

How To Be A Pop Star...

...In Five Easy Lessons

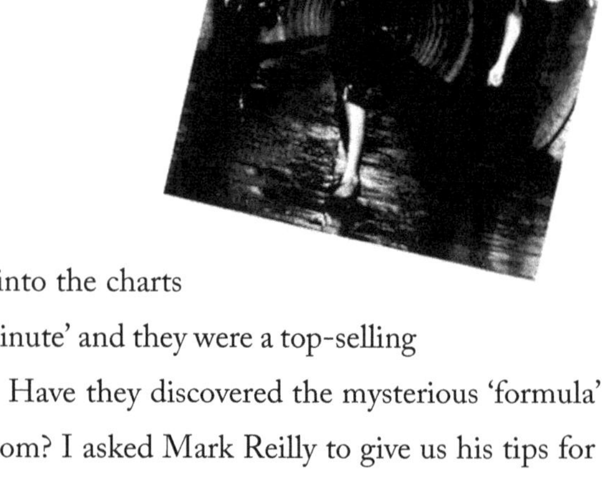

When Matt Bianco released their first single, 'Get Out Your Lazy Bed', they became pop stars almost overnight. Success seemed to have come so easily that you might be forgiven for thinking that almost anyone could manage to have a hit at the first attempt.

But the second hit wasn't so easy to come by. They released other singles that disappeared without a trace. It looked as though they'd never get into the charts again. And then, finally, they came up with 'Half A Minute' and they were a top-selling act once more. Have they learnt from their mistakes? Have they discovered the mysterious 'formula' for success? ... and anyway, what is the secret of stardom? I asked Mark Reilly to give us his tips for the top...

Music

The first thing any budding pop star needs to do is to be able to play or sing pop music. This is a step which some groups overlook and still manage to be successful. But, if in doubt, it's probably better not to take any chances - so get yourself an instrument and start learning.

I taught myself to play guitar from a book when I was sixteen. I've never been all that great at it but I do use the guitar a lot for writing songs. I only started singing when I left Blue Rondo à la Turk to form Matt Bianco a couple of years ago. I think I've always had a reasonably good voice, but I've still got a few things to learn about singing, which is why I've started taking lessons.

I'm not trying to learn how to change the sound of my voice, but I am trying to master correct breathing and projection. I have to do exercises and scales. A lot of people damage their voices because never done all the groundwork. Some singers go out on tour, belting it out every night so that by the end of the tour they haven't got a voice left at all.

Performance

The next big step for any would-be star is to get yourself in a group. It's all very well practising endlessly in your dad's garage, annoying the neighbours, but you'll never get yourself a wall full of gold discs until you get yourself out in public.

I used to bash away in the garage with my friend, Tim. By this stage I'd managed to learn about three chords on the guitar and felt this was plenty to get myself into a punk band. So that's exactly what I did.

Of course, no new band will make an impression unless they're original. So we wrote our own songs. They were terrible songs. But at least they were *original* terrible songs. We got our first gigs simply by going along to pubs and students' unions and saying 'Book us.' When they said 'No.' We'd say, 'We're cheap.' Sometimes it worked. Sometimes it didn't.

Later I was asked if I'd like to audition for a new group called Blue Rondo à la Turk. I did and I got the job.

Confidence

Everyone is nervous about performing. After a while the nerves wear off a bit, but in the early days they can be a big problem. The secret is to act confident even if you're scared to death.

I felt a right twit when I started doing lead vocals with Matt Bianco. When I was with Blue Rondo I was able to hide behind my guitar or do the occasional 'Boop', for backing vocals. It's actually more nerve-wracking to play live performances when you've already released some records, as we have, than it is when you're a completely unknown group. You can get away with murder when nobody knows what to expect. But now that people know Matt Bianco records, there's no way I'll be able to sing a bum note without the entire audience knowing about it. Help!

IMAGE

The secret of getting the right image is simply to dress the way you like. Another important part of image is to get across your personality. You can dress anyone up in anything and they can look terrible. But if the style reflects the personality you will look good.

I get all my clothes made up by a tailor. He knows the style I like and he makes exactly what I want. Amazingly, it's often cheaper to have clothes specially made for you than to buy similar quality things off the peg.

A lot of the big groups at the moment have awful images. They look like cast offs from 'Dallas' - no names mentioned, but Wham! and Culture Club are groups who wear things I wouldn't be seen dead in.

SUCCESS

Success is a very 'hit and miss' business, obviously. Our first single, 'Get Out Your Lazy Bed' was a big success, but our second one, 'Creeping Out The Back Door' wasn't.

In fact, for a while we had a horrible feeling that we were going to end up as just another one hit wonder. And then we put out 'Half A Minute' and, thank goodness, our luck changed.

Every group wants to be successful but it's one of those things that you can't really predict. 'Sneaking Out The Back Door' was very big in Italy and Spain, for example, and another single, 'Whose Side Are You On' was big in Holland. But they did nothing in Britain.

If I could only work out why certain songs are big in some countries and flop in others I could be the next Frank Sinatra. As it is, I'll just try to come up with songs I like and keep my fingers crossed that lots of other people like them too.

The bad side of success in that it brings with it lots of hard work and lots of disappointments. The first success makes any failures all the worse. But then, looking on the bright side, having a failure makes the next success all the better. And I suppose that's what makes a life in pop music so exciting.

HEAVEN 17

THE SKY'S THE LIMIT ..SAYS GLENN GREGORY

'**Ian and Martyn are leaving Heaven 17,**' Glenn Gregory tells me when I meet him, 'Which means that from now on it's going to be just me. We've already got some tours planned so I'm going to have to look for some other musicians to form a group.'

At this point I begin to feel an uncomfortable sensation of having heard something like this once before. After all, it was only just over a year ago, back in October 1980, that this very same Ian (Craig Marsh) and Martyn (Ware) split from another group just before a major tour, leaving the lead singer, a certain Philip Oakey, to try to piece together a new band to take the show on the road.

Of course, we all know what happened to them. But as for Messrs. Ware and Craig Marsh — you'd think that they would have learnt to hang onto something while the going was good. So why do they seem so keen on repeating history by uprooting themselves once again from a group of their own creation?

'Well, this time it isn't really a proper split,' Glenn assures me, 'Not in the sense that they split from The Human League, at any rate. It's just that, with Ian and Martyn becoming more and more involved with other recording projects for their company, BEF (the British Electric Foundation), they haven't got the time any more to go on tours and things. So we decided it would be better for me to take over the group myself.'

When I spoke to him, Glenn still had no idea what form the new Heaven 17 would take or exactly how many instrumentalists would be brought in to replace Ian and Martyn. One thing he was sure about, though, was that the new version H 17 was going to be Big. . . very BIG!

'Ideally, I'd like it to be enormous,' he told me, 'a huge force of musicians spread out all over the world, all of whom can be drawn on at any time — just like the network of spies they used to have in "The Man From UNCLE" programmes on TV. I was a member of UNCLE when I was a kid and I had a card that said "You may be called on at any time". I used to stay up late at night waiting to be called. But I never was. So now I'm going to make up for that by setting up my own organization and letting other people wait for me to call them!'

Apart from the somewhat perverse thrill of wielding this god-like power over his far-flung 'Empire', Glenn believes that if he is able to keep changing the group's line-up, then the music which they create will remain fresh and exciting. 'People stagnate when they carry on doing exactly the same thing all the time,' Glenn says, 'And that's true not only of music, but in all walks of life.

Although Glenn readily admits that his 'solidly working-class' background has strongly influenced his approach to song-writing, he does not like to be thought of as a 'political' musician.

While it is true that Heaven 17's song-lyrics do attempt to comment upon political and social issues more often than most other groups do — '(We Don't Need

This) Fascist Groove Thang', 'Penthouse and Pavement', 'Play to Win', etc. — Glenn is quite insistent that the music is meant mainly for entertainment and any 'message' in the songs is incidental. He just writes about subjects which he (or Ian or Martyn) happens to be thinking about at the time.

'At the moment it seems to me an utter waste to fill out songs with all those old "in and out of love" lyrics. Though I could imagine us doing a song like that if I'd just been through a heavy romantic affair which had broken up. 'But if people want to listen to the words, that is a sort of added extra, really. When we perform live, all I want is for people to enjoy themselves, really enjoy themselves. 'Heaven 17 will only be performing in clubs where people can dance. I want the live show to be really entertaining. Though, because it's in clubs, we won't be able to make the show too lavish.

'I mean, it would be nice to have a swimming pool on stage, full of two hundred girls, but, for the time being, I think we might have to settle for something a bit less adventurous — a couple of bed-sheets on the back wall, maybe, to project slides onto. Or then, I could go to a nightclub to look for a couple of girls to dance with us. Or has someone else done that already? You know, that group, what are they called — "The Human" something? They think of everything, don't they!'

'You see so many people getting themselves stuck for year after year, into doing jobs that they hate. I did it myself for a while. Before joining the group I was a photographer working in advertising. I didn't enjoy it because advertising is as boring as hell. When I got the chance of joining this group I threw in my job straight away without any hesitation.

'Within the first few months of doing that I was so short of money that I had to sell my camera to get enough cash to live on. Even today I'm earning less than I was as a photographer. But, at least, what I'm doing now is a damn sight more exciting.'

THE SKY'S THE LIMIT

'Ian and Martyn are leaving Heaven 17,' Glenn Gregory tells me when I meet him. 'Which means that from now on it's going to be just me. We've already got some tours planned so I'm going to have to look for some other musicians to form a group.'

At this point I begin to feel an uncomfortable sensation of having heard something like this once before. After all, it was only just over a year ago, back in October 1980, that this very same Ian (Craig Marsh) and Martyn (Ware) split from another group just before a major tour, leaving the lead singer, a certain Philip Oakey, to try to piece together a new band to take the show on the road. Of course, we all know what happened to *them*. But as for Messrs. Ware and Craig Marsh – you'd think that they would have learnt to hang onto something while the going was good. So why do they seem so keen on repeating history by uprooting themselves once again from a group of their own creation?

'Well, this time it isn't really a proper split,' Glenn assures me. 'Not in the sense that they split from The Human League, at any rate. It's just that, with Ian and Martyn becoming more and more involved with other recording projects for their company, BEF (the British Electric Foundation), they haven't got the time anymore to go on tours and things. So we decided it would be better for me to take over the group myself.'

When I spoke to him, Glenn still had no idea what form the new Heaven 17 would take or exactly how many instrumentalists would be brought in to replace Ian and Martyn. One thing he was sure about, though, was that the new version H17 was going to be Big . . . *very BIG!*

'Ideally, I'd like it to be enormous,' he told me, 'a huge force of musicians spread out all over the world, all of whom can be drawn on at any time – just like the network of spies they used to have in "The Man From UNCLE" programmes on TV. I was a member of UNCLE when I was a kid and I had a card that said "You may be called on at any time". I used to stay up late at night waiting to be called. But I never was. So now I'm going to make up for that by setting up my own organisation and letting other people wait for *me* to call *them!*'

Apart from the somewhat perverse thrill of wielding this god-like power over his far-flung 'Empire', Glenn believes that if he is able to keep changing the group's line-up, then the music which they create will remain fresh and exciting.

'People stagnate when they carry on doing exactly the same thing all the time,' Glenn says. 'And that's true not only of music, but in all walks of life.

'You see so many people getting themselves stuck for year after year, into doing jobs that they hate. I did it myself for a while. Before joining the group I was a photographer working in advertising. I didn't enjoy it because advertising is as boring as hell. When I got the chance of joining this group I threw in my job straight away without any hesitation.

'Within the first few months of doing that I was so short of money that I had to sell my camera to get enough cash to live on. Even today I'm earning less than I was as a photographer. But, at least, what I'm doing now is a damn sight more exciting.'

Although Glenn readily admits that his 'solidly working-class' background has strongly influenced his approach to song-writing, he does not like to be thought of as a 'political' musician.

While it is true that Heaven 17's song-lyrics do attempt to comment upon political and social issues more often than most other groups do – '(We Don't Need This) Fascist Groove Thang', 'Penthouse and Pavement', 'Play to Win', etc. – Glenn is quite insistent that the music is meant mainly for entertainment and any 'message' in the songs is incidental. He just writes about subjects which he (or Ian or Martyn) happens to be thinking about at the time.

'At the *moment* it seems to me an utter waste to fill out songs with all those old "in and out of love" lyrics. Though I *could* imagine us doing a song like that if I'd just been through a heavy romantic affair which had broken up.

'But if people want to listen to the words, that is a sort of added extra, really. When we perform live, all I want is for people to enjoy themselves, *really* enjoy themselves.

'Heaven 17 will only be performing in clubs where people can dance. I want the live show to be really entertaining. Though, because it's in clubs, we won't be able to make the *show too* lavish.

'I mean, it would be nice to have a swimming pool on stage, full of two hundred girls, but, for the time being, I think we might have to settle for something a bit less adventurous – a couple of bed-sheets on the back wall, maybe, to project slides onto. Or then, I could go to a nightclub to look for a couple of girls to dance with us. Or has someone else done that already? You know, that group, what are they called – "The Human" something? They think of *everything*, don't they!'

45

DURAN DURAN

GOING THEIR OWN WAY

HUW COLLINGBOURNE CHATS TO DURAN DURAN ABOUT STARDOM, SOCIETY AND HOT, STEAMY NIGHTS WITH... **SIMON LE BON**

When their first single, 'Planet Earth', brought Duran Duran to the public's attention in the spring of 1981, a lot of people dismissed them as a mere sub-Spandau rip-off trying to cash in on the New Romantic craze.

'People seem to feel much happier if they can fit you into a category.' Nick Rhodes thinks, 'In fact! the only similarity between us and Spandau was that we both used to wear frilly shirts . . . and I suppose our drum sounds were quite similar too.

'But nobody makes these comparisons any more, thank goodness. They can see now that we are very different groups. And anyway, Spandau have now moved on to the new fad - imitation funk. We don't want to be any part of that.'

It soon becomes clear when talking to these lads that they would hate to be thought 'a part' of *anything*! When Nick Rhodes and John Taylor formed Duran Duran in 1978, they were determined that the band should have a unique and unmistakable identity. To this end, the music which they played was, at first, intentionally very up-to-date and experimental.

'Most people found it totally unacceptable,' Nick explains, 'because we had a clarinet player, a rhythm box' two bass guitars and no lead guitar. It was very obscure. We enjoyed it at the time but eventually we felt we had to move on to something a bit more substantial.

Changes

During the next couple of years the band went through numerous changes before arriving at the present line-up with John Taylor (21) on bass, Andy Taylor (21) on guitar, Roger Taylor (21) on drums (none of whom, incidentally, are related to each other), Nick Rhodes (19) on synthesiser and Simon Le Bon (23) as vocalist,

'The thing which makes us all work well together,' Nick says, 'is that we are five very different individuals. We all have quite strong personalities. Sometimes this fact means that there's a lot of tension between us, because we all have conflicting ideas. But that only seems to make us work better.'

Simon agrees. 'I'm not a "team sport" type of person,' he says, 'And this is the only team I've felt happy in - because we're all as good as one another and have each other's respect even when we disagree quite strongly.'

Gay?

By their own standards, one of the greatest measures of Duran Duran's success is the broad cross-section of people who come to their concerts. No longer are their audiences restricted to a fashionable young 'Futurist' following, but include everybody from 'twelve-year-old schoolkids to forty-year-old executives.'

'At our last gig in Sweden the audience were practically all gay skinheads'. Nick tells me. 'It struck us as very peculiar because in Britain we don't seem to attract skinheads at all.'

And gays?

'People used to think that Duran Duran had gay overtones and must. therefore. have an enormous gay following But they discovered that we had more of a girl following than a gay one.

'I suppose we have adopted a certain flamboyance which, for some reason, has always been associated with gay people, and not everybody finds that easy to accept. But again this is just an example of people's attempts to separate everything into categories, to say *this* is gay but *that* isn't. It seems very silly to me because, after all, gay people are I exactly the same as everybody else in everything but their sexual habits. The people who insist on this sort of separation must have very closed minds.'

Simon has even more pronounced views on the way that people attempt to categorise one another in recognisable social or sexual groups.

'Society continually tries to make people conform rather than to develop their individuality,' he says, 'It begins when you are very young and you have to try to fulfil your parents' expectations. After that you are forever pushed into becoming a part of various institutions: school, church, college and so on.

'Institutions like that cater only for he majority. They're inflexible and cause an awful lot of pain and damage.'

Rebellious

When Simon was a child his parents wanted him to become an actor and even now he continues to feel some resentment at their attempts to push him in this direction irrespective of his wishes.

'I started doing TV commercials when I was six,' he says, 'Amongst other things I was the boy with the dirty shirt in the Persil advert.

'Then, in my teens, I went through a period of rebellion. I finished A-levels, was a complete failure and went to Art School for a year. I got sick of that because I don't like Art students very much - they're so insular. Besides, it was just another institution.'

But aren't there a lot of restrictions inherent in being famous?

Nick answers that: 'The reverse is true,' he says, 'Fame brings you lots of nice extras - being recognised in the streets, seeing yourself on TV, doing interviews with your favourite magazines, going to a nice restaurant and having the manager turn round to you at the end of the meal and saying "Oh, you don't have to pay for that" . . . silly little things like that!'

Alone

But what about the loss of privacy? Surely there must be times when you wish you could just go out into the street like everybody else without being continually recognised by people you've never even met.

'People in Britain are, on the whole, very considerate,' Simon reckons, 'Even when they recognise you they don't always encroach on your territory. They realise that there are times when you want to be alone.

'From time to time reporters find out things about me I wish they wouldn't. I can't blame them for wanting to do it, though, There's nothing I'm particularly ashamed of and it doesn't worry me what I other people think of me.

'Slowly I'm getting used to the I fact that it is no longer possible for I me to have a private life. You have to make a conscious decision to I give that up when you become a public figure. You don't have any *right* to a private life.'

Society

Some people might think that rather a high price to pay for fame. After all, isn't there some part of *everybody's* life which they would rather keep separate from the world at large?

'Only my sleep,' Simon says, 'I sleep a lot. And it can be a bit of a trial when girls phone up at three o'clock in the morning and want me to spend a few hours talking to them or to go out for a drink or something.

'But, to put it in perspective, I think the loss of my privacy is relatively unimportant. What is much more serious is the way in which society affects everyone's personal freedoms. I believe that we are now coming to a point where everything will start to become more and more institutionalised, making people less free to be themselves and live in the way they wish to - or else it may start becoming *de*-institutionalised, increasing people's freedoms. It could go either way - it's all dependent upon economics and party politics.

'These are the things people should be worried about. But it - wouldn't concern me at all whether or not Bridget Parnell of Islington chooses to write to a popular newspaper about "My Hot And Steamy Nights With Simon on Le Bon" – I'd find that quite funny!'

DURAN

Going their own way

Huw Collingbourne chats to Duran Duran about stardom, society, and hot steamy nights with Simon Le Bon.

When their first single 'Planet Earth' bought Duran Duran to the public's attention in the spring of 1981, a lot of people dismissed them as a mere sub-Spandau rip-off trying to cash in on the New Romantic craze.

'People seem to feel much happier if they can fit you into a category,' Nick Rhodes thinks. 'In fact, the only similarity between us and Spandau was that we both used to wear frilly shirts . . . and I suppose our drum sounds were quite similar too.

'But nobody makes these comparisons any more, thank goodness. They can see now that we are very different groups. And anyway, Spandau have now moved on to the new fad – imitation funk. We don't want to be any part of that.'

It soon becomes clear when talking to these lads that they would hate to be thought 'a part' of *anything*! When Nick Rhodes and John Taylor formed Duran Duran in 1978, they were determined that the band should have a unique and unmistakable identity. To this end, the music which they played was, at first, intentionally very up-to-date and experimental.

'Most people found it totally unacceptable,' Nick explains, 'because we had a clarinet player, a rhythm box, two bass guitars and no lead guitar. It was very obscure. We enjoyed it at the time but eventually we felt we had to move on to something a bit more substantial.'

Changes

During the next couple of years the band went through numerous changes before arriving at the present line-up with John Taylor (21) on bass, Andy Taylor (21) on guitar, Roger Taylor (21) on drums (none of whom, incidentally, are related to each other), Nick Rhodes (19) on synthesiser and Simon Le Bon (23) as vocalist.

'The thing which makes us all work well together,' Nick says, 'is that we are five very different individuals. We all have quite strong personalities. Sometimes this fact means that there's a lot of tension between us, because we all have conflicting ideas. But that only seems to make us work better.'

Simon agrees. 'I'm not a "team-sport" type of person,' he says. 'And this is the only team I've felt happy in – because we're all as good as one another and have each other's respect even when we disagree quite strongly.'

Gay?

By their own standards, one of the greatest measures of Duran Duran's success is the broad cross-section of people who come to their concerts. No longer are their audiences restricted to a fashionable young 'Futurist' following, but include everybody from 'twelve-year-old school-kids to forty-year-old executives.'

'At our last gig in Sweden the audience were practically all gay skinheads,' Nick tells me. 'It struck us as very peculiar because in Britain we don't seem to attract skinheads at all.'

And gays?

'People used to think that Duran Duran had gay overtones and must, therefore, have an enormous gay following. But they discovered that we had more of a girl following than a gay one.

'I suppose we have adopted a certain flamboyance which, for some reason, has always been associated with gay people, and not everybody finds that easy to accept. But again this is just an example of people's attempts to seperate everything into categories, to say *this* is gay but *that* isn't. It seems very silly to me because, after all, gay people are exactly the same as everybody else in everything but their sexual habits. The people who insist on this sort of separation must have very closed minds.'

Simon has even more pronounced views on the way that people attempt to categorise one another in recognisable social or sexual groups.

'Society continually tries to make people conform rather than to develop their individuality,' he says. 'It begins when you are very young and you have to try to fulfil your parents' expectations. After that you are forever pushed into becoming a part of various institutions: school, church, college and so on.

'Institutions like that cater only for the majority. They're inflexible and cause an awful lot of pain and damage.'

Rebellious

When Simon was a child his parents wanted him to become an actor and even now he continues to feel some resentment at their attempts to push him in this direction irrespective of his wishes.

'I started doing TV commercials when I was six,' he says. 'Amongst other things I was the boy with the dirty shirt in the Persil advert.

'Then, in my teens, I went through a period of rebellion. I finished A-levels, was a complete failure and went to Art School for a year. I got sick of that because I don't like Art students very much – they're so insular. Besides, it was just another institution.

But aren't there also a lot of restrictions inherent in being famous? Nick answers that:

'The reverse is true,' he says. 'Fame brings you lots of nice extras – being recognised in the streets, seeing yourself on TV, doing interviews with your favourite magazines, going to a nice restaurant and having the manager turn round to you at the end of the meal and saying "Oh, you don't have to pay for that" . . . silly little things like that!'

Alone

But what about the loss of privacy? Surely there must be times when you wish you could just go out into the street like everybody else *without* being continually recognised by people you've never even met.

'People in Britain are, on the whole, very considerate,' Simon reckons. 'Even when they recognise you they don't always encroach on your territory. They realise that there are times when you want to be alone.

'From time to time reporters find out things about me I wish they wouldn't. I can't blame them for wanting to do it, though. There's nothing I'm particularly ashamed of and it doesn't worry me what other people think of me.

'Slowly I'm getting used to the fact that it is no longer possible for me to have a private life. You have to make a conscious decision to give that up when you become a public figure. You don't have any *right* to a private life.'

Society

Some people might think that rather a high price to pay for fame. After all, isn't there some part of *everybody's* life which they would rather keep separate from the world at large?

'Only my sleep,' Simon says. 'I sleep a lot. And it can be a bit of a trial when girls phone up at three o'clock in the morning and want me to spend a few hours talking to them or to go out for a drink or something.

'But, to put it in perspective, I think the loss of my privacy is relatively unimportant. What is much more serious is the way in which society affects *everyone's* personal freedoms. I believe that we are now coming to a point where everything will start to become more and more institutionalised, making people less free to be themselves and live in the way they wish to – or else it may start becoming *de*-institutionalised, increasing people's freedoms. It could go either way – it's all dependent upon economics and party politics.

'These are the things people should be worried about. But it wouldn't concern me at all whether or not Briget Parnell of Islington chooses to write to a popular newspaper about "My Hot And Steamy Nights With Simon Le Bon" – I'd find that quite funny!'

25

ABC

A COUPLE OF YEARS AGO IT SEEMED ALMOST IMPOSSIBLE TO GET AWAY FROM ABC - THEY WERE EVERYWHERE, ON THE RADIO, ON TV IN THE MAGAZINES. THEY'D HAD A STRING OF HITS WITH SONGS SUCH AS 'POISON ARROWS' AND 'THE LOOK OF LOVE', AND THEY'D ALSO PRODUCED TWO TOP SELLING ALBUMS 'THE LEXICON OF LOVE' AND 'BEAUTY STAB'. AND THEN, ALL OF A SUDDEN, THEY DISAPPEARED. NO RECORDS, NO VIDEOS, NOTHING. NOW, AS SUDDENLY AS THEY DISAPPEARED, THEY'VE COME BACK AGAIN. BUT WITH A NEW LINEUP. I SPOKE TO SINGER, **MARTIN FRY**, AND ASKED HIM WHAT'S BEEN GOING ON IN THE PAST YEAR OR SO...

Well, Martin, so where have you been all this time?

In 1983 we did a huge tour based around 'The Lexicon Of Love'. We took a sixteen piece band around with us and the whole thing involved lots of tuxedos and glamour. We ended up playing in Tokyo though we'd set our sights on playing Las Vegas until they said they wouldn't have us because they already had Dean Martin and Sheena Easton there, so what did they want us for?

When we came back we did a bit of recording but, by this time, Steve Singleton felt he'd done as much as he wanted to with the group and so he left. In January 1981, Mark White and myself then started setting about re-forming the group.

We held auditions in the YMCA in Sheffield. We listened to about 125 drummers, about 80 keyboard players and 75 bass-players, all of which proved fruitless.. We decided that being able to play en instrument well was less Important then having lots of good ideas, so we asked a couple of old

friends, Eden and David Yarritu, to have a go at playing drums and keyboards. They'd never played in any groups before but that doesn't really matter. As long as you've got the ideas you can program a machine to make the sounds for you.

You were always a very stylish group. How's that style changed now?

Now we're even more stylish. When we started out we were all living in Sheffield and penniless and we were in love with the American Dream. We wanted to be in the world of 'Dallas' and 'Dynasty'. But now, having seen so much of America, we've realised how useless that all is. We've fallen in love with the United Kingdom. As a result we've become a lot more flash and flamboyant.

Have you deliberately re-planned your style or has it just changed naturally?

Style is something you've either got or you haven't. It's something that follows you around. You can be stylish in the nude.

Is it true that you flushed your gold lame jacket down the toilet?

Oh yes. I'd just spent seventy-five nights in the thing and I was pretty sick of it. I thought it was about time I got something new.

You've toured all over the world with ABC. Where (apart from Sheffield) is your favourite place?

Japan. Tokyo is an a outrageous city. It's what Barnsley will be like in fifty years time. They show cartoons in the street from huge hoardings, They've got the newest, highest skyscrapers in the world. It's just a mass of neon and modern technology.

Do you like to be surrounded by technology in your everyday life?

You mean things like compact disc players, answering machines, vending machines in the kitchen and electric toothbrushes in the bathroom?

Well, no, I haven't got any of those things. I don't really like the microchip inside my home. There's too many things that can go wrong with them and I can hardly even wire a plug.

It's funny that I should love the hi-tech world of somewhere like Tokyo. I think if I stayed there for more than three weeks at a time I'd probably go crazy, though.

Have you ever appeared on any Japanese pop shows?

Oh yes. ABC were once on 'The Funky Tomato' show. It's a lunchtime pop and chat show. The Japanese equivalent of 'Wogan', I guess.

Apparently lunchtime is the peak viewing time. When we were on it I was interviewed in Japanese. They told me everything would be all right because I'd have a translator but, unfortunately we lost the translator in the crowd so I kept getting asked things in Japanese and I just nodded and said 'Yes' to everything. I must have looked a real jerk.

What are the worst experiences you've ever had on your travels?

I've had some awful flights. One of the worst was on a plane from New York to Los Angeles. It was about to take off.

The plane just began to go up into the air then it came straight back down again. The pilot told everyone to get off because there was a crack in the wing. That scared me a bit.

On another occasion I was in a plane flying above a thunder storm and we looked down at all the lightning beneath us. It was like looking into a crystal ball,

Any ambitions to perform in countries you've never played in previously?

I'd love to do some concerts in China and Russia. Maybe we'll have the chance some time. But I must say that, at the moment, my main aim is to do as much as we can in the good old U.K.

Barnsley, here we come!

The Thompson Twins

THE TINY, whitewashed room let in hardly a breath of the stagnant malarial air from the hot and dusty street outside.

The room's three occupants were growing irritable in the relentless heat. They had been locked in together for more than a week now, and they were beginning to get pretty sick of the sight of one another. And of the sound. And of the smell - yes, especially sick of the goddam' smell! ... But they had a mission to perform and nobody was going to get out of that room until the mission was completed.

"We'd gone to Egypt to be totally isolated," Alannah explains. "The old version of The Thompson Twins had just split up and now there were the three of us, Tom, Joe and myself, and we needed to get some new songs written."

I've heard of people going to great lengths in search of inspiration. But why Egypt, for Chrissakes?

"Well, you see, we've always been London based," Tom explains. "Making London-type music, for London people. It's been the bane of our lives and we wanted to make a break from that. So Egypt seemed a good place to go...

"There were no distractions there," Joe recalls. "Just flies, bad food and sand in your eyes.

"In a place like that, so.. foreign, we all seem to come together, "says Alannah, "Mind you, we do have terrible fights when we try to work together. We throw things at one another and cry. It's all very traumatic.

"But we've worked so long together that we can cope with that. We know how to manipulate one another, you see, and stick the knife in. There's no democracy in the Thompson Twins, we run it on a totally Fascist basis."

Sounds really great.

"Oh, it was," Tom assures me, "We wrote the first four songs on our album while we were in Egypt."

By now, I can see that all you globe-trotting *Flexipop*! readers are just itching to blow all your hard-earned pennies on a once-in-a-lifetime holiday on the banks of the far, exotic, fly-blown Nile.

But wait a moment-the people at Thompson's Holidays have got lots more wonderful ideas for never-to-be-forgotten vacations in ghastly surroundings.

"After Egypt, we went to the Bahamas," Alannah says, "It was all very wonderful with the sun and the sea going splosh splosh under the veranda..."

Ah yes, now that really does sound idyllic.

Thompson's Holidays!

"But we got bored," says Joe. "There was nothing to do but swim around and look at different coloured corals."

"So we came back to Britain and set up our studio in the ballroom of a mansion presided over by a crazy woman in Wiltshire," says Alannah. "That was better. It gave its a weird sort of feeling as though The Bomb might be about to go off at any moment on the other side of the hill.

You gotta give it to these kids, they certainly know how to enjoy themselves! I mean, as far as they are concerned, fun is just old hat. This year's big new leisure concept looks like being unadulterated misery, gloom and despondency.

And for the ultimate in A Really Bad Time, Thompson Holidays can recommend nothing more highly than a couple of weeks in grimy, fever-ridden Delhi.

"I went to Delhi a couple of years ago," enthuses Tom, “And l got a terrible gastric disease.

"It was so dirty there and the water was so bad that I thought I was going to die, so I asked someone to take me out of the city and into the hills where it would be cleaner and more healthy.

"I was taken to a monastery where every morning I was just carried out of a bed and dumped in a courtyard, because I couldn't even manage to walk there on my own.

"It was in the courtyard that they did the cooking. After a few days I got so bored of watching them that I started to ask about what they were doing. I learnt quite a bit of Hindi that way. I also found out all about those mysterious looking spices.

"When I got well enough to walk again, I started going to the village to buy ingredients from the merchants there, and to cook various dishes for myself. I became quite good at it. In fact, I eventually got a job as the monastery's cook!"

There you are, you see - you too could become a cook to an Indian Monastery. And you mean to say you thought working in a kibbutz was hip?

It was at this juncture in the conversation that Alannah decided that she ought to put in a word about all the myriad wonders of her homeland, New Zealand. Unfortunately, she couldn't think of any - and so we got around to discussing the Continental countries of Europe instead.

Having had two Number One clubland hits in America and also entered the charts in Britain, surely the Thompsons must now be eager to conquer France and Germany and Holland and ...

"Oh no, I'm not at all bothered about the Continent," Alannah hissed. "I mean, you've only got to go to one of those countries to see what the trouble is - they're full of bloody foreigners, aren't they."

Now there you've hit the nail on the head, Alannah.

"And don't you dare quote me on that!"

Oh, Alannah, as if I would...

TOM BAILEY of The Thompson Twins

PICKS HIS TOP AND BOTTOM 5 RECORDS...

TOP FIVE:...

1 'The Brandenburg Concertos' by J.S. Bach, performed by Walter Carlos
Walter Carlos (who is now known as Wendy Carlos) did a synthesized version of Bach - he was the bloke who did the music for 'A Clockwork Orange', which was tremendous. I'm very fond of all of Carlos's music - it puts a lot of pop groups to shame

2 'Revolution' by The Beatles
I'm as much a Beatles fan as anyone else is and we actually did a cover version of 'Revolution' so I must like it.

3 'Jammin' by Bob Marley
I'm quite into reggae and this combines good-feel reggae with quite a commercial hit, which can't be bad.

4 'Miracle Of The Fishes' by Milton Nascimento
What do you mean, 'obscure'? I've heard of him so he can't he obscure! He's from Brazil and he sings in Portuguese. He's actually done quite a bit of work with American jazz musicians and is quite well known in certain circles. The thing I really love about his records is his voice which is fantastic and quite unique.

5 'Hold Me Now' by The Thompson Twins
Well, I don't believe any pop musician who doesn't have one of his or her own songs amongst their favourites. In fact, it's very difficult to say which of our songs is my favourite because there's so much emotional investment that has gone into all of them, I think you soon find out which ones aren't your favourites, though. There are two divisions: those songs which become very dear to your heart and those which are just 'other songs'.

BOTTOM FIVE...

1 Heavy Metal (of all sorts)
I have a great intolerance of Heavy Metal Music. I especially dislike all those groups who push a sort of macho-violence image. For one thing, it's not very serious which makes it all the more worthless.

2 'Agadoo' by Black Lace
Actually, it's not really fair to Black Lace to single out that record. It's just an example of the type of music that irritates me. I'm not crazy about very thin, churned-out pop music. To say I'm not crazy about it is probably an understatement. But you wouldn't print what I really feel.

3 Any record by Leonard Cohen
He is a singer and poet who used to be very trendy years ago, back in the '70s – very turgid and miserable; and, for some reason, there are still people about who insist on playing his records even today. Whenever anybody puts a Leonard Cohen record on, I leave the room. I don't like sad songs in general. Even if they are very good I can't abide them. The same goes for films too - things like 'Cat On A Hot Tin Roof' or 'Who's Afraid Of Virginia Woolfe?'. I can appreciate they are well written and well acted but they are so depressing.

4 The music for 'Match Of The Day'
Mainly because it means that 'Match Of The Day' is about to come on TV.

5 The National Anthem
I can't claim to be Her Majesty's most devoted subject. I wouldn't say I'm an anti-Royalist because I don't think that being an anti-Royalist is important enough to put any energy into it. It strikes me that in this day and age the world should be looking for ways to break down its national barriers not to reinforce them, and the more that people think nationalistically, the less they think about the planet as a whole. There are lots of movements, as indicated by Live Aid, aimed at trying to make people see the world as one thing. The National Anthem represents outmoded ideals of Empire and Nation, suggesting that this land has inherently something better going for it than anywhere else on earth, I think it's about time that people in Great Britain started to see themselves as part of a much greater thing - namely the world.

KIM WILDE ON MEN!

THEY SAY IT'S A MAN'S WORLD. AND A QUICK GLANCE AT THE POP CHARTS WILL SHOW THAT THE MUSIC SCENE IS CERTAINLY ONE PLACE WHERE MALE STARS FAR OUTNUMBER FEMALES. BUT THERE ARE A FEW GIRLS WHO'VE MANAGED TO PENETRATE THIS MASCULINE DOMAIN. ONE OF THEM IS **KIM WILDE**. MALE POP STARS HAVE MADE QUITE A FEW HIGHLY SEXIST REMARKS ABOUT KIM OVER THE YEARS. WE DECIDED THAT IT WAS ABOUT TIME TO EVEN UP THE BALANCE A BIT AND GIVE KIM THE OPPORTUNITY OF MOUTHING OFF ABOUT SOME OF THE MEN ON THE POP SCENE...

BOY GEORGE

"He's a very sweet person but his image doesn't appeal to me at all. Initially it was great because he was outrageous, outlandish and shocking. But now it's just rather tacky and boring. Not my cup of tea at all."

SIMON LE BON

"Duran Duran have made some quite good records but I find Simon himself rather unconvincing and affected. I was with him once and he started talking to me and I'd read exactly the same words ten minutes ago in a magazine. Poor bloke. I think he needs a break. Send him on holiday, I say."

Kim Wilde and Simon Le Bon later went on a 'blind date' (organized by *Flexipop*!). Surprisingly, they got on very well together in spite of the fact that Simon did not wear a tight dress for the occasion!

GEORGE MICHAEL

"I used to like Wham! when they first started out. They were quite sweet. But now their act has become so overblown. I don't know why George Michael seems to be building up some sort of James Dean image. He doesn't need to do all that because he writes good songs that stand on their own merit. I don't like the way he looks now. I really can't see what girls see in him."

MICHAEL JACKSON

"He's a brilliant performer. He looked a lot better a few years ago though. He's beginning to look rather emaciated these days. I've never met him but, if you believe whet you read, it appears that he's losing touch with reality. Maybe that's not true though. Maybe half of those stories are made up. He hardly ever talks to the press which I find pretty impressive. He just says everything through his songs."

PAUL YOUNG

"He's got a great voice. I've met him a few times and I like him a lot. What more can I say?"

HOLLY JOHNSON

"I think all of Frankie Goes To Hollywood look great - but especially Holly. He's certainly one of the most charismatic performers about at the moment. He's very *very* attractive. He's the most attractive person in this list, as a matter of fact. He's not really the standard pop pinup, but then I don't go for that type of man anyway. Holly is far more interesting than all these other pop stars with gleaming white teeth, suntans and swept-back hair."

DIVINE

"I like that glam' image. I used to love all the old Rockers such as Marc Bolan, Sweet, Slade and Gary Glitter. I think Divine has some of that spirit. Reel silly stuff which appeals to me. He's got a tremendous sense of humour. As a personality, Divine is far more convincing than Simon Le Bon. Maybe Simon Le Bon should try a tight dress on!"

PRINCE

"A great performer. Very exciting. He was absolutely ridiculous in the film 'Purple Rain', but at least he was ridiculous with style. His image, sort of camp and butch at the same time, works very well, I think. I like paradoxical things like that... I really mean what I said about Simon Le Bon in a dress. It'd do wonders for him!"

80S TIMELINE...

May 18th, 1980. In Washington State, in the Northwest of the USA, the long dormant volcano, Mount Saint Helens, began a devastating eruption which produced a 60,000 foot column of ash which darkened the skies for over 160 miles. Fifty-seven people were killed and trees were burned and flattened for miles around.

May 5th, 1980. Britain's elite SAS (Special Air Service) stormed the Iranian Embassy in Knightsbridge in a bid to rescue hostages being held by terrorists. Viewers watched the operation live on TV as the SAS officers scaled the balcony and blew in an armoured window to gain access to the Embassy. The 19 surviving hostages were rescued and four of the five terrorists were killed.

July 17th, 1980. Ex-Hollywood actor and one-time Governor of California, Ronald Reagan, becomes the Republican Party's presidential candidate.

November 7th, 1980. Actor, Steve McQueen dies due to a heart attack following an operation.

November 19th, 1980. The TV series *Dallas* comes to a dramatic end as we discover who shot JR (yup, I know, but I'm not telling...)

November 4th 1980. Ronald Regan is elected President of the United States of America.

December 8th, 1980. John Lennon (40) is killed by Mark David Chapman outside the Dakota building in Manhattan where Lennon was living. Lennon was shot five time at point-blank range with a .38 revolver. Later it is discovered that Lennon had signed an autograph for Chapman earlier that same day.

March 30th, 1981. President Reagan is shot in the chest by a 25-year old DJ, John Hinckley III, as he leaves a Washington hotel. The bullet misses his heart by three inches and lodges in a lung.

April 29th 1981. Peter Sutcliffe admits that he is the so-called Yorkshire Ripper who killed 13 women over a four year period in the North of England.

May 13, 1981. Pope John Paul II is shot four times as he blesses crowds in St Peter' Square in Rome. Police arrest a 23 year old Turkish man, Mehmet Ali Hagca. The Pope recovered after treatment in hospital and later publically forgave his assailant.

July 29th, 1981. Prince Charles marries Lady Diana Spencer in Saint Paul's Cathedral. The wedding is watched by an audience of over 700 million people around the world.

April, 1981. Argentina invades the Falkland Islands ('Las Malvinas') which are British territory. Britain responds by sending a Royal Navy Task force to take back the islands.

June 14, 1981. British forces take full control over the Falkland Islands and Argentina surrenders.

December, 1982. Director Stephen Spielberg releases the film, *ET (the 'Extra Terrestrial;'.*

June 9, 1983. Mrs Margaret Thatcher is re-elected as British Prime Minister. She first came to power in May, 1979.

January 27, 1984. Michael Jackson is seriously burned while filming a TV advertisement for Pepsi Cola. The 25 year-old star was showered by sparks from a firework display which set fire to his hair.

November 7, 1984. US President, Ronald Regan (73), wins a second term of office with a landslide vote going 59% in Regan's favour.

March 11, 1985. Mikhail Gorbachev becomes leader of the Soviet Union – at 54 he is the youngest man ever to attain this position,.

July 13, 1985. Live Aid, a massive international rock concert aimed at raising money for starving people in Africa, is televised across the world. It is thought that more than one and a half billion people tune in to watch stars such as David Bowie and Queen performing on stage at the Wembley Stadium in London and the JFK Stadium in Philadelphia.

January, 4, 1986. Thin Lizzy singer, Phil Lynott, dies from pneumonia and heart failure. He has been in hospital receiving treatment for kidney and liver infections related to excessive drink and drugs use over the Christmas period.

January 28, 1986. The American space shuttle, Challenger, explodes on take-off, killing all seven members of the crew, including the first ever 'citizen astronaut', school teacher, Christa McAuliffe.

April 30, 1986. The world learns that a Russian nuclear reactor at Chernobyl in Ukraine is on fire.

February 22, 1987. Artist and film director, Andy Warhol dies during an operation.

June 12, 1987. British Prime Minister, Margaret Thatcher, is re-elected for her third term of office.

November 8, 1988. George Bush is elected President of the USA.

December 21, 1988. A Pan American jumbo jet, Flight 103 flying from Heathrow to New York, explodes in mid-air and crashes into the small Scottish town of Lockerbie, killing all 259 passengers and 11 people on the ground. Two men, accused of being Libyan agents, were eventually charged with planting a bomb on the plane.

Feb 14, 1989. Iranian leader, Ayatollah Khomeini, issues a decree or 'fatwa' calling for the death of British author, Salman Rushdie, whom he accuses of writing an 'anti-Islamic' novel, *The Satanic Verses*.

www.ingramcontent.com/pod-product-compliance
Ingram Content Group UK Ltd.
Pitfield, Milton Keynes, MK11 3LW, UK
UKHW051129260726
13967UKWH00010B/2936

9 781471 601781